Psychic Women

PSYCHIC WOMEN

*Exploring the Supernatural
with six great psychics*

ANTOINETTE MAY

FOR JOHN

Revised Edition 1984

First published by Chronicle Books under the name
Haunted Ladies.

Library of Congress Catalog Card Number:
84-81350

ISBN: 0-915689-03-0

Hickman Systems
4 Woodland Lane
Kirksville, MO 63501

Printed in the United States of America

Contents

Psychic Women

Introduction

If anyone had suggested even a year ago that I'd be interviewing dead people, I'd have questioned his sanity.

An atheist since early childhood, I had as little use for ghosts as I had for angels. They were merely archetypical symbols—curious objects of interest for Jungian shrinks or Jesus freaks—with scant appeal to an untroubled realist like myself. What couldn't be seen, tasted or smelled clearly did not exist. I'd always known that.

As a teenager, my mentor had been Omar Khayyam. Remember:

"Oh threats of Hell and hopes of Paradise!
One thing is certain and the rest is Lies;
The flower that once has blown for ever dies."

This view fit very well into the trendy, timely world of the journalist that I became. Today's news today and tomorrow the same news that teams of writers, editors, and printers fight to obtain, analyze, and produce becomes a handy wraparound for someone's garbage can. The analogy to life was obvious. Enjoy today fully, because *there is nothing else out there.*

And I did enjoy today very fully. Within a relatively short time, I had actually lived out many of my girlhood fantasies. I had found challenging work, a measure of recognition, periods of high adventure, a few storybook romances, clever, kindly, and highly supportive friends. It was a very good life; right here, right now, and that was all I cared about.

So how did it all begin? What twist or turn of fate plunged me—a very skeptical newspaper editor—into the murky, mist-shrouded world of the occult?

A *prophesy* what else! Returning from a rather hectic assignment in Athens, I decided to stop off in London for a few days to relax and visit friends. London is my favorite city in the world—one that has beckoned to me many times since childhood in both a physical and an intellectual sense. The people, the history, the literature of London, of all of England, has always exuded a very special magnetism—a crazy, scary, happy madness, not unlike love. I wonder a lot about that *now*—a consistent pull, a sense of comfort, exhilaration, and a familiarity to a place where I have no ancestral ties. But *then* I had no thought other than to enjoy a brief carefree holiday.

On the spur of the moment, C. J. Marrow, a long time friend, decided to fly over and join me. "I don't know why I did it," she confessed later. "I'd been to London once before and didn't care much for it, just another big city. But this time it's so different. I really think it has to do with you somehow. This is surely your place. I seem to be seeing it all in different layers, overlays of time with you superimposed in some way." I merely shrugged, unable to fathom her meaning, but pleased that she was enjoying herself.

Much of C.J.'s time was spent rushing about festooned with cameras taking color shots of the city for the travel pages of her newspaper. Then one day she ventured, "London *is* famous for its mediums. Don't you think we should try one?"

In my naivete, I equated mediums—channels of communication between the earthly world and the world of the spirit—with fortune tellers. My only experience had been with the latter, grimy gypsies using vague threats of doom to sell prayer candles or madeup matrons in garish costumes at charity bazaars promising the inevitable "tall, dark stranger." But to my surprise, I found myself agreeing. Why not? In London, do as the Londoners do.

A friend gave us the name and number of Douglas Johnson which meant nothing to us at the time. Much later we were to learn of this gifted sensitive's prestigious connection with the College of Psychic Studies. So, unaware of Johnson's nationwide prominence as "resident medium" of the college, we blithely called for an appointment. "We're leaving in two days for Dublin, could we drop by tomorrow?" I asked.

There was a slight pause. Pushy Americans, he was probably thinking. "I rather doubt it, I'm booked three months in advance," was the frosty reply.

Three months! My newspaper nose was twitching. The man must have something to be that busy. Curiosity aroused, I persisted, "Couldn't you squeeze us in for just a few minutes?"

Another pause and the sound of pages turning. "Well, yes, I believe I can," he replied in a rather surprised tone. "I have my appointment book here, and it seems that there's been a cancellation. If you could both come at four tomorrow, I'll do a double sitting for you and your friend. I'm afraid there won't be time for anything more."

The following afternoon found us in Mr. Douglas' cozy, cluttered living room. He was a distinguished looking man, an aging James Bond type, gray-haired, super casual; but still urbane. Douglas proved a friendlier, warmer person than he'd sounded on the phone.

"My! You've been here before, haven't you?" he greeted me.

"Why no, I'm sure we've never met," I answered, puzzled.

"No, I mean to London, to England."

"Oh, yes, several times."

"No, my dear, I mean *before* those times. In other lives."

Ho hum, reincarnation, we're going to play that game, I thought, a little disappointed. I'd half hoped for a few facts, names or events concerning my real life, things that could be known and verified, not fancies about some mythical past. But it *was* funny that he'd fixed on London . . . my stream of consciousness ended abruptly as he suddenly centered on the more recent past.

"You were married once to a man named Robert. You're divorced now but remain good friends." This was all quite true and so were the other very personal and quite specific details that followed.

It seems important to mention here that I told him nothing about myself nor did C. J. I made no comments, asked no questions and remained impassive until the very end.

"You're a writer," he informed me, and then waved a finger in gentle disapproval. "My dear, I can see your desk at home. It's long, rather narrow and simply covered with papers. (It was.) You're doing many different things. Short columns for newspapers, magazine articles—too many things really. You're scattering yourself and your energies. (I was.) But you're going to stop all that soon. When you return home you will be writing a book. You will concentrate on it."

"Oh, no!" I spoke for the first time. "I have no plans to write a book. I don't even have a subject in mind or know a publisher."

"The publisher knows *you*. The plans are being made now. They will be revealed when you return to the United States."

Back home two weeks later, I found a stack of mail waiting; but the first letter that I opened was from the publisher of this book with the suggestion that I drop by to discuss the possibility of writing a book. The result of our conversation was *Haunted Ladies*.

This experience did leave me somewhat stunned. I had never met this publisher before or had any previous contact with his company. He had heard of my work through a mutual acquaintance and talked about the book idea with him during the time that I was in London.

But one minor miracle does not a believer make. *Haunted Ladies* as I originally perceived it was to be a very light, whimsical, even cynical approach to mediumship. Yet as the work progressed, as I came to know and to respect Eileen Caddy, Betty Bethards, Rosemary Brown, Irene Hickman, Thelma Moss, and Anne Armstrong, my skepticism faded. For all their surface differences these six women—super women of the supernatural—have a common message of comfort and courage relative to us all. Each in her own way has produced not merely vague ideas but actual evidence of communication with a world beyond the narrow dimensions of the known. The message shared is not one of old fashioned moralizing laced with wishful thinking, it is the result of actual communication with another form of life.

In recent years a variety of people have been drawn to the theory of reincarnation. Some have invested it with a game concept. "I was more important than you were," is very popular. Its appeal is obvious. Who wouldn't prefer a shortcut to importance? I'd personally be delighted to discover a link with Nell Gwynn, George Sand or Nellie Bly, any of the audacious women who somehow managed to emerge from the morass of anonymity, leaving their heelmarks triumphantly upon the hide of history.

But far more important is the possibility of finding the purpose in a universe of unbroken continuity where birth is not the beginning nor death the end. While an acceptance of karma still carries with it an incentive to be "good" as heaven once did, it also replaces apparent madness with meaning. Such a concept supplies answers to questions both individual and universal, explaining the random cruelty of life.

Personally, I find the second chance aspect of reincarnation immensely appealing. The mistress in me enjoys the romance, the homemaker appreciates the tidiness. What many have done with their second chance is an intriguing subject for another book. The gifted Swedish author, August Strindberg, believed himself to be the spiritual evolvement of Edgar Allen Poe. George Patton, the famous World War II general, thought himself an incarnation of Napoleon, recalling intricate details of battles once fought and long forgotten. None of this would have surprised Napoleon who frequently declared himself to have been Charlemagne reborn.

The late comedian, Charley Weaver (in private life, Cliff Arquette), while walking about the historic battlefield at Gettysburg, recalled a past life as a surgeon in the Union Army. Searching the Gettysburg Cemetery, he came upon what he believed to have been his gravestone from that distant life. The name inscribed there was *Charley Weaver*. Coincidence? Or was Arquette drawn in some mystical fashion to select a name from a previous life to be his stage name in this existence? Curiously, Arquette's son, Louis, believes that he too played a part in the Civil War—but on the Confederate side.

Where is Charley (or Cliff) now? one wonders. Possibly he's getting ready to interrupt the classical hour at Rosemary Brown's house. A few jokes between symphonies might liven up the repertoire. If the idea seems absurd, consider the impressive list of believers. They include Franklin Roosevelt, Henry Ford, Thomas Edison, and even pragmatic Benjamin Franklin.

While viewing the likely prospect of death from the trenches of France during World War I, Winston Churchill wrote his wife, "Do not grieve for me too much. I am a spirit confident of my rights. Death is only an incident and not the most important which happens to us in this state of being." Churchill and Anne Armstrong may one day have lots of notes to compare.

Since coming to know Mrs. Armstrong and the others, I have also become "a spirit confident of my rights." A new dimension to reality has emerged within myself and as a result I have been forced to accept a totally new philosophy of life. Having studied, investigated, and analyzed the life and work of each of the inspired women whose stories comprise this book, I am impressed that each has achieved an integration of the practical and the spiritual unknown to most of us. By a fusion of these two, they have literally achieved miracles.

The implication—to me at least— is that when we live totally in the sensory reality, we live out only a fraction of our possibilities. The rest has become blocked. To remove this crippling obstruction, one may require the "pick and shovel work" of an Irene Hickman.

Have I changed since writing this book? Yes and no. If anything, I find myself living more in the moment than ever before. I feel more open to new ideas, new people, new experiences. I'm literally ready for anything. I have a deeper sense of wonder and delight in being human and alive because I have no idea what tomorrow may bring. But of one thing I am certain: *there is plenty out there and one day I will discover it all.*

Somewhere in the vast unknown I'm certain that my girlhood guide, Omar Khayyam, has discovered that while the flower may die, the tree goes on and on and on. Who knows, Omar may even have returned as Voltaire, who wrote: "It is no more surprising to be born twice than once; everything in life is resurrection."

Nothing is impossible.

Palo Alto, California, 1975   Antoinette May

Eileen Caddy

A Garden Where the Plants Do the Talking

Is the old god Pan alive and piping in Northern Scotland?

A surprising number of people believe that he is. They also attest to communion with obliging fairies who will produce, if not a pumpkin coach, then a forty-four pound cabbage.

They tell of a Garden of Eden thriving only a short distance from the Arctic Circle. Besides roses blooming in the snow and eight-foot delphiniums buffeted but un-bowed by North Sea squalls, they speak of manifestations of light and power linking all forms of life in harmonious achievement.

The legend of Findhorn, Scotland's secret garden, will delight some while confounding others. Its setting—a lonely area of fog-drenched seacoast not far from the spot where the three witches prophesied to Macbeth that he

Eileen and Peter Caddy

would be Thane of Glamis and Cawdor—is eerie enough for a Gothic horror story. Yet this wonder tale began prosaically enough in November of 1962 when three friends, Eileen and Peter Caddy and Dorothy MacLean, suddenly lost their jobs.

Since all had experience and expertise in hotel management, their abrupt termination as employees of a luxury lodge in Forres, Scotland was totally unexpected. Each felt certain that it was merely a temporary thing, a misunderstanding that would quickly be resolved in their favor. But what to do in the meantime?

Though receipts at the hotel had trebled during their tenure and the establishment had risen to four-star status, they had been asked to vacate within four hours. It was a shocking, disheartening experience, a cruel, unnerving blow to the self-esteem of each, yet Eileen met this sudden vicissitude with quiet equanimity. Far greater tragedies had prepared her for any crisis. Ten years before she had divorced her husband in order to marry Peter and, as a result of the ensuing scandal, lost her five children, her friends, relatives and social position. The terrible ordeal had left her with a survivor's reserve of courage, the ability to act on faith alone and to shrug in the face of meaningless convention.

During this earlier period of painful soul searching, Eileen and Peter had driven away from their home in London hoping to find respite in the peaceful countryside. Stopping at Glastonbury, they entered the historic sanctuary. As Eileen sat quietly, attempting to compose herself, to accept the loss of everything previously held dear, a voice spoke to her. *"Be still and know that I am God,"* it told her. *"You have taken a very big step in your life. Listen to Me, and all will be well."*

Eileen looked about her in utter amazement. She and Peter were completely alone. Raised in the highly rational, orthodox Church of England, she was totally bewildered by the phenomenon. But her skepticism vanished as a sense of peace descended upon her. From that moment on, Eileen has never been without this feeling of oneness and purpose and has received divine messages which have directed the course of her life. All sorts of insights—both practical and spiritual—were received in this fashion and dutifully recorded in a notebook.

Having meditated daily for years, Eileen found it only natural to seek answers outside herself to enable them to cope with the unexpected dilemma. No one was very happy with the guidance she received. "Ugh!" they groaned collectively upon hearing that they were to move to a nearby caravan (trailer) park, a barren patch of sand and gorse beside the Firth of Moray on the northeast coast of Scotland.

Peter knew the spot well, having driven past many times while taking hotel guests to a nearby yacht club. "The park was the very last place that any of us would have elected to go," he admits today. " 'Imagine living in a dump like that, cheek to jowl with one another,' I'd often said. It had appeared to us as excessively crowded and far from beautiful."

Grumbling to themselves, the three adults, accompanied by the Caddy's three boys, ages five, seven, and eight, wheeled a small caravan into the space assigned them. It was slightly apart from the others, adjacent to a rubbish heap piled high with rotting garbage, tin cans, brambles, and broken bottles. Surrounded on three sides by the sea, the derelict area with its sand dunes and rabbit holes was constantly swept by winds of gale force.

"Of course it will be for only a short time," each attempted to reassure the others. But as the cold, damp winter enveloped them with its chilling mist and seemingly endless bleak days, their repeated efforts to find employment ended in failure.

Accustomed to the luxury of large hotels, each felt acutely the cramped, primitive conditions and lack of privacy. "Did we get on each other's nerves? I should say so!" Eileen laughs today. "All of us were used to sumptuous five-course meals served in a massive dining room with wine and brandy. Now we were subsisting on eight pounds a week in welfare payments. There were no conveniences. I had to do all our washing in the bathtub. The clothes were spread all over the caravan to dry during bad weather—which was most of the time."

An elegant, silver-haired woman, she smiles ruefully, recalling those early months when she would rise at midnight to meditate. Only partially protected from the winter winds by many layers of clothing, Eileen would sequester herself for hours in the caravan park's toilet—the only spot where she was certain to find isolation and tranquility. In this frigid setting, hands numb with cold as she gripped her notebook and pen, she was guided to plant a garden.

Without prospects and almost without funds, the group still remained hopeful of leaving the area. Surely only a quick crop was needed—lettuce and radishes perhaps, nothing that would take long to grow, for they would soon be moving on.

But, as the work began, even growing lettuce appeared a hopeless task. The ground contained no soil, merely fine sand and gravel. To make matters worse, no one in the group had ever gardened before or had any idea of how or where to begin. Not one had so much as sown a single seed.

What happened next, the Findhorn residents believe is literally a fairy tale come true. They call it *manifestation*.

According to Eileen, manifestation is like a reverse prayer. "We don't really ask for things," she explains. "We're told that we're to have them—usually through my Guidance. Then we begin to very specifically make plans. My Guidance once said:

> 'Think abundance all the time and never for one second think lack in any form. Accept My vast storehouses and all that is within them; they are there

waiting to be used. Use all of everything; give constant thanks and recognize My hand in everything.'"

"It would have been easy to say the soil was useless for anything—as indeed it was," Dorothy pointed out. "But recognizing the necessity of growing strong, healthy plants we focused all our physical energies and positive thoughts into all we did. Amazingly, the garden took shape."

First a wood fence was erected and inside its protection a few seeds were planted. Since little money was available, the three adults and three children were entirely dependent on the principles of manifestation for survival. They were not disappointed; their faith literally bore fruit. The necessary ingredients to turn sand into soil were given to them and, as one source of supply ran out, another immediately opened up.

One day the novice gardeners were informed by a neighbor that a large quantity of damaged cement had been dumped just down the road. It was easily salvaged and soon utilized as a patio and walkways. A large clump of grass was discovered and became the start of a compost pile. A friend who owned a riding stable donated a quantity of manure. Seaweed was collected on the beach, and a nearby distillery supplied peat moss and cummings—a barley residue which is a potent fertilizer.

One evening while hiking, Peter found a sheep that had become entangled in a fence and was hanging upside down. He released the animal and notified the farmer, who was so grateful that he delivered a truckload of manure the following week.

Soon loads of grass cuttings were donated. A shop gave them old potatoes and vegetables that could not be sold. The day the gardeners realized they needed straw for covering the compost heaps, a neighbor dropped by with a bale that he had found by the roadside.

Eileen watched with some amazement as her husband, who had once been a Royal Air Force squadron leader and command caterer in the Burma campaign and later the manager of a luxury hotel, became a master manure mixer. Strong, authoritative, he greeted this new challenge with typical humor, vigor, and resourcefulness.

At about the same time, assistance on another level was offered. On May 8, 1963, Dorothy MacLean sat down to meditate and received the following message:

"The forces of nature are something to be felt into, to be stretched out to. One of the jobs for you is to feel into the nature forces such as the wind, feel its essence and purpose for Me, and be positive and harmonize with that essence. It will not be as difficult as you immediately imagine, because the beings of these forces will be glad to feel a friendly power. All forces are to be felt into, even the sun, the moon, the sea, the trees, the very grass. All are part of My life. All is one life. Play your part in making life one again, with My help."

Dorothy interpreted this as a delightful invitation to walk in the wilderness. Strolling among the golden gorse bushes that border the rocky seacoast, she felt herself becoming one with a stream of power which seemed to urge her to be open to the realms of nature and view them sympathetically. "It seemed a little presumptuous to attempt to tune into the sun or the moon," she admitted. "Finally I decided to experiment with a pea, they're my favorite vegetable."

Holding a pea pod in her hand, Dorothy tried to tune in to its essence and got an immediate answer from the spirit of the pea which confided some of the secrets of the vegetable kingdom. She believes their communication was made possible through an attunement rather like telepathy.

Plants have no objection to being eaten, the pea spirit assured her. "Eating can bring unity between the two worlds. We understand humans and human motives but do not always approve of them. You think slugs are a greater menace than man," it accused her, "but slugs are a part of the order of things. Only man takes without gratitude."

Dorothy wondered if slugs give thanks. "They are not that evolved," the pea explained, "but—unlike man—they follow the force field without destroying the order of things. Man's thoughts affect all other orders of life. As you become more spiritually attuned, perfection will be brought into form in the plant world."

The pea, which was a kind of world soul or spokesperson for all peas—not merely for the individual pod that Dorothy held—advised her on how and where peas should be planted, how often they should be watered, and suggested that vegetables be eaten as soon after picking as possible for best value.

Dorothy perceived the divine deities within the plant world as *devas*, which means "shining one" in Sanskirt. "They are really angels, but that word has such a limited meaning in English," she explains.

Shortly after this exchange during her daily meditation, Eileen received guidance that they were not to

Cabbages growing around the trailer

attempt to grow flowers in the garden. Instead they were to concentrate all their energies on cultivating every conceivable fruit, vegetable, and herb native to Scotland.

During the first year, sixty-five different vegetables were grown, twenty-one varieties of fruit, and forty-two types of herbs. As each was planted, Dorothy attuned herself to the appropriate *deva* and welcomed it into the garden. When special information was needed, the *deva* was contacted again. Once when some newly transplanted lettuce seemed to be failing, she received the following advice:

"We do not approve of transplanting. It weakens the plant forces. To man it is convenient, to us it is inconvenient and weakens our charges. Nature's methods of a prodigious mass of seeds, from which only the strong survive, ensures the best for the plant. In the best of all worlds, man should sow seeds more thickly than is needed and then thin out by destroying those whose life forces he can see are weak. He is then aiding Nature, and Nature in turn will produce health for him."

When questions of a more general nature arose, the overseer of the Findhorn *devas* appeared. From this Being, whom Dorothy called the Landscape Angel, they learned that the greatest contribution man can make to a garden is the energy that he puts into the soil while cultivating it. The *devas* themselves are fully capable of producing for themselves whatever else is needed.

They were told that every person at Findhorn had a quality to give the garden—some strength, some tenderness, some love, some power, and so forth. So great was this collective contribution that they were soon harvesting forty-four pound cabbages and a broccoli of such enormous proportions that it provided food for a week and when eventually pulled out was almost too heavy for Peter to lift.

Unfortunately the Caddy family and Dorothy were not the only ones to thrive on the garden's abundance. Moles were now industriously engaged in digging a network of tunnels beneath the rows of vegetables that had been so laboriously cultivated. Delighting in the succulent roots, they had begun to ravish the prize plants.

Dorothy believes that she was able to plug in to the essence of the moles, to their group soul, and then explain to them the importance of the garden to the humans solely dependent upon it. "Food from the garden is all we have," she pointed out. The moles apparently got the message. Though they continued to proliferate in the surrounding area, none were found in the garden.

By this time Peter had built a small annex to the trailer, a wooden shack where Dorothy could sleep at night. At first the new-found privacy seemed delicious but soon Dorothy discovered that she was not alone. Rats were visibly gnawing their way upward from the makeshift foundation below her. During the day they remained silent and hidden. At night she could hear them squeaking and scratching beneath the floorboards.

Trying to overcome her own instinctive fears, she attempted to reason with them on a calm, rational level. "I work very hard during the day," she explained. "I simply must sleep at night. I can't promise what any other human will do—although I shall certainly try to influence his or her behavior; but if you will leave me in peace, I will never attempt to trap or poison you or do anything to harm you in any way." From this time on, Dorothy reports, the rats were totally silent.

"I would occasionally see one scampering down a path but it certainly didn't menace me in any way," she says. "I even used to fancy they wiggled their ears at me in a friendly, conspiratorial manner. Anyway, the point is, they kept their word. It was a kind of gentlemen's agreement and certainly gave me a new respect for the animal world. Moles and rats have every reason to feel distrust or even hostility toward man. What have we ever done but try to exterminate them completely? Now it appeared that they were bending over backward to accommodate to human needs. It seemed proof that the divine spirit within all creatures is far greater than surface animosity."

The Findhorn garden continued to flourish. Brussels sprouts grown there were the only ones in the area to survive a plague of cabbage root grubs which eat away at plant roots. Bushels of black currants were harvested while the crop failed elsewhere in the county.

Then in June of 1964 Eileen recalls that the county horticultural adviser was given a sample of soil for analysis. The man was aghast at the gritty, sandy substance that Peter presented to him and stated that the sorry soil would require a dressing of at least two ounces of sulphate of potash per square yard. When Peter explained that he did not believe in artificial fertilizers and preferred to use compost with only an addition of wood ash, the horticulturist replied that this would be totally impossible. Nothing could grow in such a base, he insisted, before reluctantly departing with the sample.

Six weeks later he returned, bringing with him the results of the soil analysis which had been conducted in Aberdeen. To his amazement, the tests had revealed no deficiencies at all in the soil sample. All the necessary elements were present.

The horticulturist was so impressed that he asked Peter to take part in a broadcast emanating from the Findhorn garden with himself as master of ceremonies and joined by an experienced gardener who used conventional methods of gardening, chemical fertilizer, etc.

"Peter consented," Eileen recalls. "We felt at the time that the world wasn't yet ready for *devas*, but Peter did take advantage of the opportunity to make a plea for a return to the balance of nature. He had a strong case. The proof of the pudding was to be found in the eating and the horticultural adviser had seen for himself our remarkable vegetables along with the results of the soil analysis."

A new and even more startling dimension was added

when the Findhorn gardeners made the acquaintance of R. Ogilvie Crombie, a scholarly gentleman in his seventies. Crombie, who had been a student of physics, chemistry, and mathematics at the University of Edinburgh, believes himself to be in direct communication with Pan. A representative of the god first appeared to him, Crombie told Eileen, in the Botanical Gardens of Edinburgh in March of 1966. "Suddenly," he related, " 'I saw a figure dancing around a tree nearby, a beautiful little creature about three feet tall. I noted with astonishment that it was a faun, the Greek mythological being, half human, half animal. He had shaggy legs ending in cloven hooves, pointed ears and chin and two little horns on his forehead."

Hardly did Crombie have time to accustom himself to the emissary before Pan himself appeared before him. Pan, Crombie says, manifested late one evening as he was strolling by the National Gallery. Once again it was a faun-like creature with horns, pointed ears, and cloven hooves, but this was a large figure, taller than himself and radiating a tremendous power. Pan warned Crombie that the nature spirits—of which he is lord—are fast losing interest in the human race as they have been made to feel that they are neither believed in nor wanted. "If you humans think that you can get along without us—just try!" he challenged.

Crombie, obviously a believer, assured Pan of his faith and insisted that he needed all the help he could get.

The Findhorn gardeners needed it too. In the spring of 1967 Eileen received guidance that the garden was to be extended and made into a place of beauty as well as utility. This meant planting trees, shrubs, and flowers. "The barren soil was considered to be quite unsuitable for the growth of deciduous trees, but Pan promised us his help and that of his subjects should we decide to attempt to grow trees and shrubs," Eileen explained later.

"It was the end of April and already very late in the season for planting; but, on looking around a nursery, Peter was inspired to get a large chestnut tree together with an assortment of other trees and shrubs. These were planted in the same sandy soil and—to make matters worse—a dry summer followed. Pan, however, kept his promise. The growth of the chestnut tree averaged fourteen inches—an astonishing amount in view of the adverse conditions. The size and color of the flowers growing entirely in sand were truly remarkable. One delphinium grew eight feet and had enormous blossoms. Certainly it was not due to any experience on the part of the gardener!"

In analyzing the phenomenon later, Crombie deplored the fact that the concept of Pan was so totally unacceptable to many. "It's unfortunate that, due to the materialism of the nineteenth century and the subsequent disbelief of the present age, man tends to dismiss anything that cannot be seen, touched, and analyzed in a laboratory as nonexistent—so these wonderful beings are considered to be pure imagination.

"There is hope," he conceded, "in the fact that nuclear physics is being led to the possibility that matter may have no real existence, but is a build-up of whirls or vortices of energy and that material things which are supposed to be the only true reality have no actual existence. Does not the ever-growing enthusiasm of the reading public for J.R.R. Tolkien's *Lord of the Rings* point to a returning belief in nonphysical beings? Of course, people will say that there is all the difference between fiction and real life. But what is so-called real life? What is reality?"

Yet even in paradise problems can develop, as Peter found to his dismay a few weeks later when he cut back flowering gorse bushes to make way for his young fruit trees.

"Dorothy was terribly upset at their being cut down just when they were in full bloom and accused Peter of butchering the plants," Eileen recalled. "He retorted that she was going rather too far, since every time a lawn is mowed plants are in a sense butchered. The action seemed entirely reasonable to him since our primary concern at the time was to provide ourselves with food."

The following weekend Crombie arrived and was almost immediately accosted by a group of highly irate elves, who demanded to know why their homes had been wantonly destroyed. Convinced at last, Peter walked among the remaining gorse bushes apologizing for his ignorance. "How could he not believe Crombie's message?" Eileen asks. "Despite all odds we had succeeded in an area where everyone else had failed. Somehow something had communicated with Dorothy telling her what to do and when. Those instructions had never failed us. Now if Crombie saw angry pixies—whether the rest of us saw them or not—it certainly behooved Peter to make peace with our benefactors. How could we doubt that something beyond ourselves was maintaining us?"

Later Dorothy received the following message:

"Cooperation with the nature spirits is a two way affair. It is not enough for man to believe in them and ask for their help. He must also respect them and avoid doing anything to give offense.

"Certain flower spirits left because of what seemed to them to be wanton mutilation of the plants they tended by removing the blossoms. Remember that flower spirits are concerned with beauty and resent any violation of it. Flowers may be picked to beautify the home. They will not resent this if it is explained to them. If flowers have to be pulled off in order to stimulate growth of leaves for food, this should be done before the petals have opened out. Once they have done so they may have become the dwelling places of tiny little beings whose presence and whose goodwill ought to be cherished, not repulsed. Weeds in a garden are growths in the wrong places and can be removed. But this, as far as possible, should be done before any flowers open out."

This advice has been scrupulously followed, and today one can often see Findhorn gardeners talking earnestly to the plants explaining why they must be cut, thinned, or even removed.

Pan later reappeared to Crombie and explained that if the cooperation of the nature spirits was desired, a part of every garden should be set aside as a refuge for them.

In explaining his conception of the hierarchy of the garden, Crombie identified the *devas* as the architects. They design the archetypical patterns that trees and plants will take. They also channel energy. The nature spirits are the builders who follow the plans and transform the energy. The material growth takes place within this ethereal counterpart and conforms to it.

"Of course, this is all nonsense to the orthodox scientist who will maintain that the whole plan of a tree or flower is in the seed, in the genetic code, in the DNA molecules," he admits. "But can we be certain that the DNA molecule itself has no ethereal counterpart with perhaps elemental beings working within it? Could it duplicate itself without such a counterpart?"

The following year Sir George Trevelyan visited Findhorn. Sir George is the son of the aristocratic cabinet minister Sir Charles Trevelyan and nephew of the historian G.M. Trevelyan. An ardent scholar and educator, Sir George lists Prince Philip among his many former students and is credited in England for having pioneered the concept of adult education.

As a member of the Soil Association of Scotland, Sir George first came to Findhorn at the insistence of several other soil experts who were at a loss to explain the garden's fantastic success. Finding the phenomenon so remarkable that he urged an open-minded, unprejudiced investigation, Sir George agreed with other soil specialists who had stated unequivocally that the high quality of flowers and vegetables growing in sand simply could not be explained merely by the use of good compost.

"If anyone believes that he can achieve these results by normal methods, let him try in the next sand dune," he challenged, adding hopefully, "This would make an interesting experiment."

Yet even as he spoke new changes were already under way. For the first few years the Findhorn gardeners had lived as hermits. "We were building deep spiritual foundations, learning patience, persistence, and perseverance," Eileen explains. "Perhaps we needed solitude to allow these qualities to take root."

It was gradually beginning to dawn on the small group that there must be some underlying purpose for their exile. The fact that none of them had been successful at finding jobs—try as they might—seemed to indicate that they were already involved in some mysterious mission that necessitated their stay at Findhorn. Though the Caddys and Dorothy MacLean continued to live quiet, contemplative existences totally removed from village life, word of their amazing horticultural success began to spread. A series of commercial gardeners and soil experts were drawn to Findhorn, hoping to discover the secret of its abundance.

After visiting Findhorn in June of 1968, Armine Wodehouse of the Radionic Association wrote:

"I had a certain amount of experience myself in soil treatment having run a commercial market garden in Wales for twenty years where I used both organic and orthodox chemical methods. I had also had experience in treating soil radionically with the use of instruments, having treated both my own soil and that of other gardens for some years.

"The first thing that struck me at Findhorn was its exposed situation. It was open to winds from every quarter with virtually no shelter or windbreak. The second point that struck me was the texture of the soil which appeared to be pure sand on the top of which had been spread compost as a dressing. In view of these two factors the crops produced were, in my opinion, little short of remarkable."

The following month another expert, Elizabeth Murray, wrote:

"I had the pleasure of visiting the Findhorn Bay Caravan Park garden on July 18, 1968, having been invited as an independent organic gardener and member of the Soil Association.

"The garden lies on the southwest of a shallow sand dune and the soil consists of a layer of fine slightly earthy sand under the turf on top of a variable depth of shingle. Any part which is uncovered must be mulched at once or the entire topsoil would vanish in the wind.

"I was impressed at once by the vigor and radiant health of everything which was growing—trees, flowers, fruit and vegetables—far beyond the ordinary. The compost was plentiful but not of very great quality, I thought. It was activated by some farmyard manure and watered with the 'night' bucket from one of the caravans. All the produce treated with this compost—mulch only, on top of the sand and shingle—was superb. I have never seen anything to compare with it anywhere, not merely for size but for quality and flavor as well. I am quite certain that such results could not have been produced on that soil by good husbandry and compost only.

"It seemed certain that there must be another factor at work which required explanation. The explanation given to me by Mr. Caddy—although entirely strange to me—I must admit I found convincing."

Professor R. Lindsay Robb, a man who had spent the first twenty-five years of his life on his father's farm and then gone on to receive degrees from the agricultural college of Glasgow University and the Scottish Dairy Institute, was particularly impressed by Findhorn. As head of the Department of Agriculture of London University, he visited the Findhorn garden on January 13, 1969.

In speaking of the experience, he admitted, "the vigor, health, and bloom of the plants in the garden at midwinter on land which is barren, powdery sand can not be explained by the moderate dressings of compost, nor indeed by the application of any known cultural methods of organic husbandry. There are other factors and they are vital ones."

During this period a subtle change was taking place at Findhorn. "For a long while no one came near us," Eileen recalls. "But after a time people began dropping by and then they would stay and stay and stay. Some never left. Among the first, of course, was our dear friend Crombie, who introduced us to the concept of Pan. Then David Spangler came from the United States, intending to spend five days with us and remaining to become a permanent member of our colony and a guiding force in its development.

"Naturally not everyone was so charmed or so charming. Many of the nearby villagers simply did not understand what we were doing. Some were truly frightened when they learned that members of our growing colony were teaching in their schools. They imagined all kinds of things and sent a team out to investigate us. It came as quite a surprise to them to find Jenny Walker, one of the most respected educators on the British Isles, living with us.

" 'Surely you're not one of these cranks?' a man asked the feisty octogenarian.

"'I surely am,' she retorted. 'What's more important than a crank? How could you get the machine going without it?'"

Eileen believes that the garden is a kind of bridge. "It's important because it dramatizes the kinship of all things. This awareness is what is carrying us forward into the New Age, a time of tremendous creativity and growth, of universal understanding," she thinks.

"Findhorn is not for everyone. One must be very self-disciplined to live without rules or regulations. We ask that people don't smoke in the dining hall, but of course they may do so in their caravans or bungalows or anywhere on the grounds if they wish. There are no restrictions against liquor—I often enjoy a glass of sherry. There are no drugs—who would want or need them here? Yet there are some who are unable to accept complete freedom. They would not choose to remain.

"In a New Age group there is no one who can say, 'I'm not that important. I can get away with this or that because it won't effect the whole.' It's only when an individual is whole and at peace within himself that he can relate creatively with others."

What appears to be new at Findhorn is that the focal point of Eileen's guidance seems to be moving from soil to soul. Suddenly, as a dispossessed family grew into a colony, the world became her garden. The principles of manifestation continued to unfold as Eileen visualized seven cedarwood bungalows occupying an area that used to be a dump—the only space left uncultivated.

"First of all, they wouldn't fit," Peter objected, "besides where would we get the money to build them?"

Nevertheless, he went ahead and bulldozed the area. After measuring carefully, he admitted that seven bungalows could be fitted into the small space. The money to build them came through totally unanticipated donations. In the same way more land was ultimately acquired and additional gardens, a greenhouse, and craft studios built.

"It has always worked in the most incredible ways," Eileen says. "Many times Peter has gone out and ordered things we needed with no money in the bank; yet in all these years there has never been an overdraft and every bill has been paid on time.

Eileen feels that *needs* rather than *desires* are met through manifestation and admits that the timetable is not always of her own choosing. "Sometimes when things don't go as fast as I would like them to, I ponder, 'Why are we blocked?' Then I realize once more that everything happening here is done according to divine plan. Expand. Consolidate. Expand. Consolidate. This seems to be the perfect pattern for us.

"I look next door at a pasture and can visualize a Findhorn market garden with a few chickens and goats. I know it will come to pass one day—of course the farmer who owns the land doesn't realize it yet; he thinks he won't sell—but he will when the right time comes."

The Findhorn concept has grown far beyond forty-four-pound cabbages. It is people who are growing now. Believing themselves to be "in the right place at the right time, doing the right thing," they are busy transforming the lessons of the garden into the world of human beings.

Among those drawn to Findhorn is Barbara Friedlander, author of the *Earth, Air, Fire and Water Cookbook*, who immediately made her presence felt in the kitchen. Barbara has been testing recipes for a Findhorn cookbook and has given up her home in New York to live in the colony. Another newcomer is Matthew, who describes himself as an ex-motorcycle thug from Blackpool, England. Matthew has taken over the garden management from Peter and now describes Pan as "me closest and most treasured friend on earth."

Nan Grey, a South African actress, is a part of the Findhorn community, as are Athena Dobbin, an interior designer from Texas, and Pat and Jim Quigley, a Canadian couple. Pat was a teacher working with handicapped and retarded children in Alberta, while Jim practiced law before going to London to work on a master's degree in international and criminal law.

"During that year in England we were moved to visit Findhorn," Jim says. "It was such a profound experience that we returned again a few months later. At about this time I was offered a position with the Canadian government in the Department of Justice. It was something that I had wanted very much as it would involve formulating social policy as the basis for new government legislation and could be a vehicle for promoting the growth of the New Age. A difficult period of indecision followed for my wife and me, but at last we concluded that it was essential that we spend more time in Findhorn to prepare ourselves for significant duties in the outside world. I declined the position, but to my amazement was told that it would remain available to me when I was ready. This seemed to us rather dramatic assurance that attunement to the divine plan will always lead to the unfolding of those openings necessary for personal growth and development."

There are nearly two hundred colonists living together on five acres of land. They range in age from newborn infants to octogenarians and include both former counter-culture activists and retired RAF officers. All appear to be very happy people working in harmony toward an alternative society. Many nationalities are represented and every walk of life. Daily activities may include teaching in the village schools or at the fledgling Findhorn University, cooking, cleaning, producing films, records, dramatic productions, weaving, potting, sand casting, and—of course—gardening.

There is none of the masochistic Spartanism often associated with religious communes. A high standard of modern comfort and cleanliness prevails. A few caravans and bungalows are owned by the community but most are the property of individuals. Emphasis is placed upon the consciousness of individuals seeking membership rather than on material contributions. Monetarily one need contribute nothing more than subsistence expenses. Ideas and energy are the basic mediums of exchange.

The philosophy of the residents transcends orthodox religion and follows highly individualized beliefs. Findhorn colonists are interested and involved in all facets of life. In 1974 their basketball team took first place in the North Scotland tournament. All the Findhorn residents seem to evidence a keen sense of humor and a down-to-earth concern with making things work.

Recently psychologist Chris Keller administered the Otis I.Q. test to the community. The results showed a Findhorn average of 124, which is 87 percent higher than the general population.

Other scores are possibly more significant. In a test designed to measure originality of thought among members, the colony might be expected to score quite low. A conforming personality was anticipated with a kind of group-think mentality. The results were completely the opposite. Scores revealed a highly independent group of strong individualists.

No one who has observed the skill with which the Findhorn men cook and clean, their pleasure in growing flowers and skill in arranging them, or their gentleness and patience with small children was surprised to learn that as a group the men showed a higher than average range of interests conventionally thought to be feminine.

The women, who readily assume roles defined as masculine by society in general, showed far fewer feminine traits than women outside the community. Findhorn women tested far lower than the norm in conformity, far higher in independence and flexibility.

Both sexes were critical of the test. "It's an obvious product of the Piscean age," a white-haired man protested. "A new creative approach to testing must be devised for the Age of Aquarius."

A small blonde complained that men and women had been forced to take different tests. "There weren't enough occupations listed in the women's test to check all the things I like to do—like carpentry, for instance. Besides, the questions were ridiculous, 'Would you like to be the wife of the president?' Why not be the president myself— if I were into that kind of thing."

A man questioned the masculine choices as well. "'Would you rather be the chairman of the board or the president?' Why not the toilet cleaner? That job wasn't even mentioned; yet it's an equally important part of life. It too must be accomplished with love, energy, and creativity if the world is to progress beyond the place where we are today."

A middle-aged woman felt that she, too, was unable to answer some of the questions. "It was as though there were two sets of answers, one for my old life and one for Findhorn," she explained. "'Who would you prefer to spend time with—a doctor? a lawyer? a lorry driver?' The lorry-driver part bothered me. Now I'd say, 'Of course a lorry driver, why not?' Before, well, I just don't know. I suppose, I'd have thought that we wouldn't have much in common. Now I know there's everything in common."

David Spangler, the young American in his twenties who came to Findhorn for five days and remained to provide a focus for its development, has introduced the concept of Findhorn as a major transitional link to the "New Age." He believes the affinity which most Findhornians feel toward one another is the result of shared past-life experiences. "If two or three or four, or whatever number of people work together consistently, they build up a team consciousness," Spangler explains. "What is released through this blending is an energy that not only is highly creative and potent but very long lasting in its effects.

"It is cumulative so that after a while people who have achieved this kind of union can come together and immediately the sparks start flying and creativity begins to pour. You may experience this with people you've never met before; but if you do feel that strong an attraction, it's because somewhere along the line in some life or other, you have already established a powerful link with them."

The submergence of individual egos into a universal consciousness that encompasses all forms of life may be the true miracle of Findhorn. The old fears and insecurities that allow social and sexual barriers to form have magically fallen away, leaving room for a new sense of personal freedom which in turn manifests itself in collective growth, happiness, and creativity.

"Someone used to the so-called 'every-day world' of wages and creditors, traffic and pollution, violence and political machinations would naturally feel an air of unreality about a place where fairies and elves and other nature spirits are accepted as normally as one would accept the police officer on the corner," David Spangler admits.

"Of course it's hard for outsiders to imagine an area where plants are acknowledged as members of the community whose interests and needs must be taken into account, where the physical, spiritual, and personal needs of the community are met—often almost instantaneously—by using spiritual laws of attraction and manifestation, where the government is by divine inspiration and guidance and where love and joy form a tangible atmosphere about the community life."

Following her nightly periods of meditation when Eileen received guidance, she would read aloud to the community the messages imparted to her at a meeting each morning which became known as "Sanctuary." Yet as time passed she became aware of a tendency among the others to see her as the only source of spiritual guidance, rather than looking within themselves for their own truths. Instinctively she felt that this kind of dependency was restricting the growth of the community.

Confirmation of this came in guidance received by her on October 20, 1971. It was the last message to be read in the Sanctuary as a regular daily event:

"My beloved, now is the perfect time for a complete change of rhythm for you. It is no longer necessary for you to receive a message from Me each day for the community and for the many. For a very long time I have gone on day after day repeating Myself; it is now time My word was lived and demonstrated. For those who have failed to take it to heart, it is there for all who need to be reminded, printed in black and white. Now is the time for living it, and the sooner this is done, the more quickly will changes come. You cannot spoon-feed a child all its life. The time comes when it has to learn to feed itself and you have to let it do so. Let go and stand back and allow all those in the community to live a life guided and directed by Me."

Of course this was a marvelously liberating moment for Eileen. Although she still continues to receive guidance that is acted upon by the Findhorn community, others are expected to assume their full share of responsibility for personal and group growth. No longer having to sleep much of the day to make up for her nightly meditations, she has been released to move into a closer, more personal relationship with other members of the community. Her presence on this more intimate level continues to exert a powerful, loving, and uplifting influence on each individual's growth.

There are no dogmas, drugs, mantras, chants, or exercises to lead Findhornians to mysticism and no gurus to keep them there. There are no formal rules or regulations, although most tasks are rotated so that everybody does a little of everything. Work, they believe, is love in action.

One woman told of spending eight months cleaning the public bathrooms. "I used to laugh about it," she said. "'Why me?' I'd ask. I'd wonder to myself, 'Will I be centered there forever?' Then one day the breakthrough came and suddenly I was cleaning with love. Scrubbing the toilet was an act of consecration."

Today she is in charge of programming Findhorn's new university. "But it really doesn't matter what I'm doing," she insists. "It's all love, all creation."

The Findhorn University is yet another development foretold by Eileen's guidance. As always, the demand preceded the space and the funds but Eileen never doubted its manifestation. On February 1, 1972, she received the following vision:

"I was shown the college and it looked like a

great egg ready to hatch. Resting over it was a wonderful being of light. The radiances were going out from this being, enfolding the egg in a glorious blanket of light. Then I heard the words, '*Be patient. Be patient. All will break forth at the right time. My timing is perfect. All is in My hands.*' Then I was aware of great movement in the egg and a loud knocking, as if a chick were ready to break out."

The chick did indeed break out. Findhorn University opened November 1973. Divided into three broad categories of humanities, art, and ecology, classes cover the Findhorn story and the spiritual laws on which it is based, attunement to oneself, communication with others, human relations, esoteric wisdom, drama, dance, music, speech, writing, and outdoor leadership. Classes are integrated with work and life in the community, for these responsibilities are considered to be an essential element in each student's education. Failure to discharge community tasks would result in suspension from classes, the idea being that the student should gain not only information but social consciousness.

Eileen feels that it is the role of a colony such as Findhorn to be a place where individuals may come and experience certain disciplines of attunement and group awareness so that they may return to the world strengthened and able to stand on their spiritual feet.

Dorothy MacLean, David Spangler, and about twenty others have left Findhorn and gone to the United States where they are busy writing, lecturing, and preparing audio-visual presentations.

Christopher Caddy, Peter and Eileen's eldest son, is now a medical student at the University of Edinburgh. As the first child to be brought up in the community to leave it, Christopher's progress has been eagerly watched by all.

In a letter to his mother written in January of 1974, Christopher said, "What I do not want to do is to Bible bash and thrust Findhorn and New Age concepts down the throats of people here. Had you ever in my upbringing forced your will upon me, I daresay I might have rejected you, and 'dropped in' on society rather than diverging in a new society. I therefore feel that in educating my fellows, force feeding is not the way, but in a slow, relentless way they can be led to view life as a much fuller and more spiritual existence, and that they are in truth cosmic beings.

"Towards the end of last term I was beginning to wonder why I had had no news from Findhorn. Was it just because I had not written? I do not think so. It was necessary in the first term for me to settle into a new environment, to manifest the correct sort of friends around me, to turn within and really ask myself where I am going.

"For too many people there is no answer to the last question. The students here are asking themselves, 'So what happens when I get a degree?' The souls around me seem to be groping, looking for a light to guide them, but are unable to see it because of tightly shut eyes. For me I know that God has a work for me to perform in the days ahead. At present I know I am in the right place and completing some of my early training.

"One of the most interesting questions to ask any student in my first year is 'Why are you doing medicine?' Some of the answers are quite astounding, especially a-mongst the girls: 'I had an inner knowing that Christ wanted me to follow this course.' Many are doing it so they can practice homeopathy and even acupuncture when they qualify, without being branded as quacks in society. They are, without a doubt, a unique bunch."

The work at Findhorn continues. Although Eileen remains the final source of guidance on all major policy matters, the community as a whole is providing through its collective attunement the new directions. The vegetables, flowers, and trees continue to be dazzling in their size and quality. Moles and insects are conspicuously absent.

Sir George Trevelyan, who came first as a skeptic and

then became a trustee of the Findhorn Foundation, has written freely of the experiment:

"What appears to be new at Findhorn is that here is a group of amateurs, starting gardening from scratch, using a direct mental contact with the devic world and in fullest consciousness basing their work on this cooperation. It is a complete partnership of the human and spiritual worlds.

"The ancients of course accepted the kingdom of the nature spirits without question as a fact of direct vision and experience. Celtic clairvoyants can still see the 'little people.' With the development of modern intellectual consciousness this knowledge has dropped out of our thinking and is often written off as superstition. An alternative explanation is that the organs of perception of the supersensible world have atrophied in modern man as part of the price paid for the evolving of the analytical scientific mind. The nature spirits may be just as real as they ever were, though not to be perceived except by those who can redevelop the faculty to see and experience them.

"Perhaps the phenomenon with which we are now concerned is simply one of many examples of a breakthrough from higher planes leading to new possibilities of creative cooperation.

"If we can accept the general concept that these beings are part of an eternal and divine world, it will be seen as a right and natural development that their leader should again show himself in recognizable form to one who had developed faculties of perception.

"If this can be done so quickly at Findhorn, it can be done in the Sahara. If enough men could really begin to use this cooperation consciously, food could be grown in quantity on the most infertile areas. There is virtually no limit if 'Factor X' can be brought into play on top of our organic methods."

Eileen does not talk of 'Factor X.' From every window she can *see* visible proof that she is in the right place at the right time doing the right thing. Fruit trees grow tall and sturdy despite the gale winds that often prevail. In an area farther north than Moscow, flowers are prolific and dazzling and vegetables abundant and delicious. It bespeaks a total harmony within the individual and with all the elements.

It also suggests that if we "talk to the trees and they don't listen to us"—it may be that we are not listening to *them*.

Perhaps it is time we did.

Rosemary Brown

New Music from the Old Masters

Rosemary Brown first made the acquaintance of Franz Liszt in 1924 when she was seven years old. Speaking slowly so as to be certain that the child understood him, Liszt explained that he had been a composer and a pianist during his life in this world.

"When you grow up I will come back and bring you music," he promised and then disappeared.

Today Liszt, who died in 1886, is a frequent guest at Rosemary's London home. Since his second visit in 1964, the famous musician has introduced a series of composers who come to dictate their work to the English widow. The group includes Bach, Berlioz, Brahms, Chopin, Debussy, Grieg, Mozart, Monteverdi, Rachmaninoff, Schubert, Schumann, and Albert Schweitzer. In recent years writers have begun to appear as well. Keats and Shelley have each dictated poems and George Bernard Shaw has a play in progress. They are all anxious that the world know they are still "alive," have retained their original gifts, and are continuing to compose.

Even at age seven Rosemary had no fear of her ghostly visitor. She wasn't even particularly surprised by Liszt's appearance. Vague recollections of spirit manifestations reach back to her second year. "A child takes a lot in her stride," she explains rather matter-of-factly. "At the very least I knew that the white-haired gentleman standing in the middle of my bedroom wearing a priest's cassock wasn't a burglar. Perhaps Liszt chose to appear to me as he looked later in life because he knew that I would recognize him from pictures and not be frightened. Almost all the school books in those days showed him as the priest he became as an old man rather than as the romantic young piano virtuoso we think of today."

Only a month or so before, Rosemary had awakened in the middle of the night to see the form of a tall man standing beside the bed looking down at her. "I sat up absolutely terrified, my heart was pounding," she recalls today. "But then as the figure vanished before my eyes, I remember sighing with relief. It was only a ghost."

The hardest part of being a child medium or an adult one seems to lie not in fear of the dead but in distrust of the living. "Oh, you know *too* much!" or "You're too far-seeing, thank you!" Rosemary's young friends were apt to say when she confided information that could not possibly have been learned in the conventional way. Most often their reactions were to withdraw from things they could not understand.

Rosemary's mother was also dismayed when her young daughter began to repeat the confidences of her spirit visitors. "You couldn't possibly know that," she accused the prattling child. "It happened long before you were born." The woman became so upset that little Rosemary felt it best to say nothing about her psychic experiences. This need for reticence put a severe strain on their

Rosemary Brown

relationship. For many years, all the while that Rosemary was growing up, there was very little communication between mother and daughter.

"Actually, what I'd heard and seen really wasn't so much," Rosemary recalls today. "It was mostly information about dead relatives or the old house in which we lived—the same house that I live in today. Since my mother had some psychic ability of her own, she may have hated to see these same qualities developing in me, knowing so well the hurt and rejection that go hand in hand with mediumship. I suppose she would have preferred for me to be just exactly like everyone else because that's the easiest way to be.

"My father was far more prosaic. He merely assumed that I'd been listening at keyholes. Then one day a former friend of his came through to me with a message. It seemed that when the two were young men this friend had cheated my father in some way and the association had terminated abruptly. He had come to me in the hope that I'd relay his apology to my father. Father was astounded. The man had died long before my birth and even my mother knew nothing of his existence. Father realized that there was no way that I could have heard anything—at least no earthly way."

Far more surprising to Rosemary than the mere existence of spirits is the idea that they should choose to appear to her. "There are so many people better qualified to help musicians than I," she sighs. "I have a very limited musical education, which meant that I was totally unpracticed in the technique of writing down notes, and I certainly knew nothing about how to orchestrate. Imagine having to worry about all that in addition to the problem of remaining in contact with beings from another world who don't always come through as clearly as one would wish!"

But then nothing about Rosemary's life has been easy. Liszt never promised her a rose garden, merely music. Though both of Rosemary's parents had been born into wealthy, rather prominent families, their fortunes had gradually slipped away. By the time that she was born, the couple was quite poor and subsisted largely from renting out rooms in their big, once fancy, Victorian home.

With the basic necessities of life so difficult to come by, no thought was given to attending concerts or buying classical records. "There was an old piano in the house—the one I still use—but Mother rarely played it," Rosemary remembers. "My father did buy a radio, but it was his private property and we children were not allowed to touch it. Even he played it rarely for we had no electricity and the batteries were expensive.

"After father died, Mother used to listen to a musical program once a week, but if the music got too heavy, she quickly switched to another station. My own inclinations toward music weren't any more classical than hers, though I did take rudimentary piano lessons briefly as a child. Later as a young woman I went to the opera with a friend from the civil service office where I worked as a secretary. I can't say that I thought much of it and wondered at the time why she was so keen on it, buying tickets and all. Actually I don't like *all* classical music even now. When I hear music played on the radio I can rarely identify the composer, even when it happens to be someone who has appeared to me."

Rosemary's fortunes did not improve with her marriage to Charles Philip Brown in 1952. Rich in love but poor in funds, the couple was forced to live with Rosemary's mother. The arrangement, originally to be only a temporary one, became permanent. Charles's precarious existence as a free-lance journalist was not improved by his ill health. Soon Rosemary was unable to work. Her time was totally absorbed with nursing her husband and caring for their two small children.

During this difficult period the ghost of Charles's first wife appeared to Rosemary, who recalls her today as a very sweet person who seemed not in the least jealous of her

husband's remarriage. "In fact, she even expressed gratitude that Charles was so well cared for and happy," Rosemary says. "Surely this proves that she had a very real love
for him and not merely a sense of possessiveness."

One evening the woman materialized while Rosemary
was sitting up with the ailing Charles. She had with her
another spirit, a young man of about seventeen whom she
introduced as their son. When Rosemary repeated this to
Charles, he quickly responded, "We had no child."

The ghost asked Rosemary to remind her former
husband of a miscarriage that she had had—which he had
momentarily forgotten. The baby, she said, had been
sufficiently developed for it to enter the spirit world and
grow up there. She added that she had named him "Mark
Anthony." When this was relayed to Charles, he almost
shouted with laughter.

Rosemary thought at first that he was laughing at the
idea of an unborn baby growing to maturity in spirit, but
then he explained the reason for his amusement. "I always
loathed the name Mark Anthony, ever since I had to learn
the long, difficult role for a school play," he said. Charles's
former wife had known this and had frequently teased him,
saying: "If we ever have a son, I shall call him Mark
Anthony." Charles worked out the child's age if he had
lived and found that he would then have been seventeen.

Not too long after this occurrence, in August 1961,
Charles died of nonalcoholic cirrhosis of the liver. Rosemary, as loving and generous as her predecessor, took
some comfort from the fact that he would be reunited with
his first family. Her own situation was very grim at that
time. Charles's protracted illness had taken every penny of
their limited savings and now she was left alone with two
small children to support, her mother having died a few
months earlier.

There seemed to be nothing that the dead Charles
could do for his family materially; but he did help them in
spirit, returning from time to time to lend support with his

astral presence. "It was very good to see my husband, who had been so pale and emaciated during the final months of his life, looking so happy and well," Rosemary says. "He was very supportive, reassuring me that the children—who were so young then—would grow up to be clever and would never give me any trouble. They are intelligent and have been very good.

"Though our son, Thomas, was not quite five at the time of his father's passing, they had been very close. After a while I noticed the small boy making all sorts of repairs about the house when things broke. 'How did you know what to do?' I would ask. 'Daddy showed me,' he would invariably answer. We all felt the presence of Charles hovering close by and it was a great comfort."

Rosemary had hoped to find some kind of secretarial work to enable her to support the family, but her children were too small to be left unattended during after-school hours. The only job available to her was working in the school kitchen. The part-time pay was meager, but somehow the family managed to subsist on it.

Three years later in March of 1964, Rosemary was washing down a table in the school cafeteria when she slipped on a carrot that one of the children had dropped. After being rushed to the hospital, she learned that two ribs had been broken and was later sent home with strict orders to do as little as possible. At first the command was easy enough to obey, for breathing itself was excruciatingly painful. But as her body began to mend, the time dragged.

Bored with knitting and reading, Rosemary sat down one day at the piano. She had not touched the instrument except to dust it in twelve years. "Suddenly I became aware of Liszt sitting beside me guiding my hands," she says. "The music being played was totally unfamiliar to me. It all seemed pleasant and natural enough. I was curiously unsurprised by his presence. Liszt didn't speak. He was simply there. I wasn't in any sort of trance and I certainly wasn't dreaming. I saw him with my fullest consciousness and recognized him immediately."

There were more visits and more and more music which Rosemary believes that she hears *clairaudiently* — clairaudience being the power to hear something not present to the ear but regarded as having objective reality. She had all but forgotten whatever small amount of piano training she had received as a child, but with Liszt's guidance she was able to play.

Then one day he reminded her of the promise that he had made some forty years before. Rosemary remembered very well, but noted that the man beside her was far younger than the original spirit and wore contemporary clothing rather than the garb of a nineteenth-century priest. Though Rosemary felt a little shy with such a famous personage, he communicated freely with her, speaking at length in English about himself and his music. "He's as easy to understand as a 'live' person," she said, "but at first I was too self-conscious to do anything but listen."

Rosemary's method of taking down the music was first to learn the pattern of notes that Liszt had used her hands to play. Then Liszt would play several bars at a time and Rosemary would memorize them before they went on to the next part. After a time she began to write down the notes. It was rough going, but fortunately Liszt was patient and considerate.

Rosemary's abilities have improved with practice, but it is still a painfully slow process. Each composer now dictates his own music, although sometimes Liszt has to facilitate the process. (He appears to be Rosemary's spirit guide as well as the organizer of the group.) "They tell me when it's a chord and then which notes make up the chord," she explains. "Then they give me the key signature and each individual note."

The problem of heavy accents and scanty knowledge of English adds to the slowness of the task. "Not all the composers speak English very well," Rosemary admits.

"That means that Liszt—whose English is excellent—has to interpret. He can speak several languages now. I don't know if he could before when he was here or not. Certainly some of the composers couldn't have spoken any English in this life, but have obviously made the effort to learn some over there. It's apparent that many have the ability to go on learning after what we call death."

Eventually word of Rosemary's amazing musical gift began to leak out. She was invited to give numerous concerts at her church. Sir George Trevelyan, the same man who investigated the Findhorn phenomenon, was a member of the church fellowship. When he heard Rosemary play, Trevelyan became so excited by the possibilities of what she was doing that he introduced her to Mary Firth, his friend and colleague, who programs and teaches musical courses at the College for Further Education at Addington Park, where Trevelyan is a warden.

Relaying Mrs. Firth's reaction, Sir George wrote: "She is left with no doubt as to the inspiration." One piece was "tremendously Beethoven"; another composition was "lovely and absolutely Chopin."

This provided a tremendous boost to Rosemary's morale. She had been working with the composers for more than two years and there was no question in her own mind of their existence or of the authenticity of their work. Yet it was reassuring to get encouragement and even endorsement from people with far more musical knowledge than she herself possessed.

Soon Monica Sims of the British Broadcasting Company had heard of Rosemary's work and presented a dignified, factual radio program centering on the music being received in this unorthodox manner. Once the broadcast was aired on October 17, 1966, newspapers picked up on the story and suddenly Rosemary was famous.

This proved a mixed blessing. Now, in addition to her work with the composers, her work at the school, the responsibility of caring for her children and large dilapidated house, she had to contend with an avalanche of mail. Not only was Rosemary's time drained but also her meager funds. Unfortunately few of those seeking information had thought to include stamped addressed envelopes to facilitate Rosemary's replies.

The composers, on the other hand, were delighted. Their grand plan was beginning to take effect. In 1969 Liszt was ecstatic when Rosemary dubiously informed him that the BBC-TV wanted to do a documentary film about her. "The program was to be the kind of grueling third-degree test that had become all too familiar," she explained. "I worried about the kind of approach these highly conservative people might take and feared they might make me out an awful fool. I dreaded it terribly, but Liszt was insistent. 'You must go ahead,' he said, 'this is what we've all been waiting for. It will be a great step forward.' " Beethoven went even further. He threatened not to dictate any more music unless it would eventually be heard by others.

"The BBC wanted me to attempt something which I have been asked to do many times. I was expected to work with one of the composers while representatives of the BBC were present. My heart did rather sink at the prospect. Some days there is no contact with the other side and I never know whether communication will take place or not."

She reluctantly agreed, but warned that it was entirely possible that nothing would happen. "All I can do is make an attempt," she said with much trepidation.

The BBC officials agreed to this and sent out two newsmen, Geoffrey Skelton and Daniel Snowman, to Rosemary's home. In a matter of minutes after their arrival, Liszt appeared to her. "There he was," she wrote in her autobiography, *Unfinished Symphonies*, "looking very calm and composed and telling me in his rather Victorian, slightly pedantic manner that he was willing to attempt to communicate a new piece of music." Liszt merely smiled knowingly when she urged him to do something "spectacular" to impress them.

Rosemary needn't have worried. Liszt was cool and professional even if she was not. His confidence gave her a measure of confidence and they plunged forward. Soon music was flowing rapidly, but it was highly complicated and Rosemary had no idea what it sounded like from looking at the notes. Finally she stopped and looked inquiringly at Geoffrey Skelton. "Do you mind if I stop and play this?" she asked.

He had no objection, but she soon found the music far too difficult for her limited skill. Then Skelton volunteered to play it. He was, she found to her surprise, an excellent pianist. After playing the notes that she had written, he turned toward her and said, "Mrs. Brown, I think you've got something there." Liszt chided her with a wry smile for her doubts and soon Rosemary was back at work writing down the music as he dictated it.

As always, it was a laborious note-by-note process, requiring tremendous concentration on her part. "I have to be so careful, because notes do sound similar," she explains. "The composers try to correct me but it can get confusing."

The composition, which Liszt named *Grubelei*, was finally completed and Skelton took it to Humphrey Searle, the world's leading authority on the music of Liszt. Searle was greatly excited by the music when he discovered a characteristic Liszt "clue." The composition could very well have been written during the last fifteen years of Liszt's life when he was experimenting with new ideas, Searle speculated. It contained a bar which resembles a cadenza in Liszt's *Liebestraum*. The bars are not identical, but Searle identified a marked similarity in construction. In *Grubelei* the right-hand notes are placed an octave higher than in the *Liebestraum*, and in *Grubelei* the passage is written in sharps and flats, but the notes are the same.

"It is typical of Liszt, characteristic of him, but still

new and fresh," Searle said. "One of its remarkable qualities was the five-four time in which it was written, something uncommon in the nineteenth century. Yet it was basically nineteenth century music, typical of Liszt. The full design of the piece is quite Lisztian."

The documentary also included two pieces that had previously been transmitted: *A Moment Musicale* by Schubert, played by Professor Malcolm Troup of the Guildhall School of Music, and a Bagatelle by Beethoven, played by Louis Kentner, a well-known English pianist.

Professor Troup told the vast TV audience: "If Mrs. Brown has not had musical education, as she claims, then the work authenticates Schubert's inspiration." Kentner, admittedly a skeptic, was forced to admit that Beethoven sounded like Beethoven and that Schubert would be extremely difficult to impersonate. "She didn't put a foot wrong," he conceded.

Richard Rodney Bennett, a symphonic composer, added that he was totally fascinated by what he had heard. "A lot of people can improvise, but you couldn't fake music like this without years of training," he said. "I couldn't have faked some of the Beethoven myself. Even if some of the pieces are bad, that doesn't mean anything. I produce lots of lousy pieces."

The experiment had been a musical triumph and a dramatic indication of soul survival, but not a particularly pleasant experience for the medium. Working with skeptical witnesses such as the BBC is very much a Catch 22 situation. "When you are working with someone the witnesses can't see, you can't help feeling a bit of an idiot," Rosemary says. "You're hearing and seeing things and responding to them and you know it looks rather odd to anyone who can't hear and see what you do. But you're an even bigger idiot sitting there waiting with no one at all to work with because all communication has temporarily ceased."

On the other hand, there are times when messages

from the other side manifest quite unexpectedly with happy results. One day during the early part of 1970 Rosemary was being interviewed in her home by three German journalists and a Hungarian photographer from the magazine *Der Speigel*. "Can you see anyone now?" one of the men asked.

Rosemary replied that she could see her own mother standing beside Liszt. Then the Hungarian, Ted Blau, spoke up, "May I ask Liszt a question?" he asked.

She agreed and Blau said something in rapid Hungarian.

"Would you ask the gentleman to repeat his question more slowly?" Liszt said to Rosemary. "I fear that my Hungarian is not very good." Though Liszt was half Hungarian, German was his natural language during his life on earth, with French a runner-up. He seems to have taught himself English, but may not have much use for Hungarian at this time, Rosemary explained to Blau. She suggested that he rephrase his question in German.

Blau apparently complied, although Rosemary had no way of knowing since she has no knowledge of either language. She saw Liszt nod. "*Ja*," he replied and then excused himself. A few seconds later he returned with a woman who was also a spirit. Rosemary described the woman, her features, coloring, and clothing in minute detail, including an unusual way the spirit had of holding her shawl with her hands on opposite shoulders. "Be sure and tell him about the shawl," Liszt urged her.

"Yes, she used to hold her shawl that way," Blau nodded. When Rosemary described the spirit as having very small feet, he answered excitely, "Yes! Yes, that's very good. It is my mother that you are describing." Blau confided that he had always felt badly because he had not been with his mother when she died. "Now I feel much better about it," he said. "I cannot thank you enough."

Rosemary learned that the words Blau had uttered first in Hungarian and then in German were a request to

Liszt to materialize his mother so that he would have some proof of soul survival.

Next to Liszt, Chopin is the most prolific of the composers. He, like the others, was first brought by Liszt, who introduced him as "my friend, Monsieur Frederic Chopin." Responding in the Old World manner popular in his lifetime, Chopin bowed politely and said, "*Enchanté.*" For a time he merely stood at the piano and watched as his friend dictated the music. Finally he commented, "She seems very nice, your English girl."

"Yes," Liszt agreed, "she is quite nice. But she is rather stupid."

Rosemary accepted this exchange with good-natured equanimity. She hoped Liszt was merely teasing—for of course he was aware that she heard every word of their conversation—but considered that perhaps she did seem rather stupid to him. "Maybe he's right," she mused, but nonchalantly continued jotting down notes. After all, she shrugged, they did seem to be stuck with one another. Stupid or not, she was all he had.

A few days later as the work was progressing nicely, Chopin commented, "Your English girl—she is not so stupid." Liszt laughed, rather like a proud father or patron. It was apparently Chopin's stamp of approval, for soon he, too, was dictating music of his own.

Rosemary describes Chopin as a natural, friendly spirit with a light, bantering manner, totally unlike the melancholy legend that surrounds him. Pleasant, unpretentious, he professes to be very angry with Rosemary's formality. "What is all this Monsieur Chopin!" he once demanded imperiously. "If you do not call me Frederic, I won't call you Rosemary," he threatened with mock sternness.

Once Rosemary had the unique opportunity to hear a tape of Chopin speaking through the famous voice medium Leslie Flint. It was exactly the same voice that she had heard many times over the years, the same pitch, the same odd, not quite French accent and the same mildly playful manner. The tape was then taken to a language expert who knew nothing of its origin. "A Slav-French accent," he declared. This seemed quite likely since Chopin was half Polish.

Mary Firth, Rosemary's early benefactor, took a number of her Chopin compositions to Dr. Hans Gal, a well-known musicologist whose specialty is Chopin. She played some of the music for him, explaining that it had been written by a student. Dr. Gal was amazed. It seemed incredible to him that anyone could have absorbed the technique and style of Chopin so completely. "Whoever wrote this must have studied Chopin and played his music all her life," he said. This, of course, was clearly impossible. Rosemary can play very little of Chopin's complex music, though her piano skills have improved somewhat since 1964.

The fact that Rosemary's piano playing has not advanced still further is certainly not Rachmaninoff's fault. This rather pedagogic spirit has tried diligently to improve her technique. He is a hard taskmaster who urges her to keep practicing chromatic sixths, which she finds practically impossible.

"If we both had more time perhaps he really could improve my playing," Rosemary speculates. "But I have all I can do to take down compositions from all those composers and then to write out neatly all the pieces that I've merely scribbled during dictation. Then there still remains my children and house to care for."

One day Rosemary had just buttoned her coat and was about to go shopping when Rachmaninoff appeared. "Oh, I can't stop now," she told him. "I simply haven't time!"

Rachmaninoff was adamant. "It's important that you take down this composition. You will need it this evening," he warned.

Rosemary was doubtful, thinking that he was merely being a temperamental genius eager to see his completed work on paper. *She* had no plans to go anywhere that evening. Finally, gentle, easygoing Rosemary put aside her own plans and yielded to his urgency. Hours later Rachmaninoff departed with a last reminder that she not forget to take the new composition with her that evening. "It is *very* important," he admonished.

Late that afternoon she received word that Leonard Bernstein was in town and wished her to have supper with him and his wife at eleven that evening in his suite at the Savoy. "Take some scores with you," she was instructed.

Rosemary was nervous at the prospect and reluctant to go, but felt that she would be letting down the composers if she didn't put in an appearance. It seemed incredible that she would be Leonard Bernstein's guest at the elegant London hotel, especially as she considered her own menial days working in a school kitchen. Rosemary felt a little like Cinderella that evening as she set off wearing various items of borrowed clothing and clutching a battered briefcase full of musical scores.

She needn't have worried. The evening was a pleasant one. Bernstein was a genial, gracious host and an enthusiastic musician. He was particularly delighted by Rachmaninoff's piece, as the composer had apparently known that he would be. When Rosemary struggled to play a Chopin selection for him, Bernstein commented doubtfully, "I don't think you could possibly have written that yourself!"

"He was so right," Rosemary recalled. "I could barely read it!"

In late 1969 a number of compositions dictated to Rosemary had been gathered and were in the process of being made into a record. On the night of January 1, 1970, she had a late-night visitor. It was Sir Donald Tovey, a British musician and composer who had died thirty years earlier. Tovey had appeared to Rosemary before and had dictated music. This time he wanted to transmit words that would be printed on the cover of the record.

Tovey's spectral appearance had a kind of irony about it. During his life on earth the man had risked his musical reputation to authenticate a Schubert violin concerto that was said to have come through on a Ouija board. His statement to Rosemary, a partial explanation of the phenomenon, appears as follows:

"As you listen to this record, you may wonder whether the music you hear is the product of Rosemary Brown's ability or whether it has indeed emanated from the departed composers who are still creating music in another world. This music itself has already called forth some admiration and some denigration (as almost any music does), but I am happy to note that the former considerably outweighs the latter. I also note that those who denigrate the music usually do so not as a result of certain exacting standards but as the outcome of a measure of skepticism.

"Many ideas have been formulated to explain the emergence of the music, but the possibility that composers of the past are still alive in different dimensions from yours and endeavoring to communicate should not be dismissed too perfunctorily. Even the most stubborn disbelievers in extrasensory perception cannot prove conclusively that there is no life after physical death and scoffers may one day find themselves faced with indisputable instances of authentic communication from those who have shuffled off to their mortal coils.

"Humanity is now moving into an age of increasing emancipation from many of its past limitations. Technical achievements and medical advances confer growing freedom from various oppressions and ills. Man's greatest problem is still himself and his orientation to his fellow beings. To understand himself fully he should become aware of the fact that he does not consist merely of a temporary form which is doomed to age and die. He has an immortal soul which is housed in an immortal body and endowed with a mind that is independent of the physical brain.

"In communicating through music and conversation, an organized group of musicians who have departed from your world are attempting to establish a precept for humanity, i.e. that physical death is a transition from one state of consciousness to another wherein one retains one's individuality. The realization of this fact should assist man to a great insight into his own nature and potential super-terrestrial activities. The knowledge that incarnation in your world is but one stage in man's eternal life should foster policies which are more farseeing than those frequently adopted at present, and encourage a more balanced outlook regarding all matters.

"We are not transmitting music to Rosemary Brown simply for the sake of offering possible pleasure in listening thereto; it is the implications relevant to this phenomenon which we hope will stimulate sensible and sensitive interest and stir many who are intelligent and impartial to consider and explore the unknown regions of man's mind and psyche.

"When man has plumbed the mysterious depth of his veiled consciousness he will then be able to soar to correspondingly greater heights."

Later the words of Sir Donald Tovey the spirit were examined to see if they matched the writing patterns of Sir Donald Tovey the mortal. David Hogarth a Scotch music critic who did the analysis, was convinced of their authenticity. Writing for the publication *Time and Tide*, he concluded by saying, "With all due respect to Mrs. Brown, I could not think for a moment that she had written it for herself."

Why was Rosemary Brown chosen to play such a significant role in this grand design? An engaging, totally unassuming person with no affectations and a keen sense of humor, she has asked herself the same question on many occasions. Long before the music came, when the spirits were merely anonymous visitors appearing and disappearing at random, Rosemary puzzled the question as a child and later as a woman. Then one day, frustrated by her own slowness at taking down the music, Rosemary asked the question of Liszt. "Why me.?"

"Because you volunteered to work with us long before you were reborn," he explained. "You agreed to be the link between us and the world when you were reborn into another aspect of life."

Rosemary was at first astonished by the revelation; but as she considered it, the plausibility of this grand scheme became apparent. She had always accepted the idea of life *after* death; why not life *before* birth?

"But why, if this is the case, wasn't I born into a family where I might have had better piano training?" she persisted.

Liszt assured Rosemary that her musical training was sufficient for his purposes. "If you had a really complete musical education, no one would have believed your claims of receiving music from us," he reminded her.

It seemed to Rosemary as she contemplated Liszt's words that her whole life had somehow been a preparation for her work of receiving the music. It was certainly true that if her knowledge of music and her skill at the piano had been greater, the general public would have been even more suspicious than it already was. It would also seem that the more she knew, the more her own ideas would have come into conflict with those of the composers. As it was, her musical mind was little more than a blank piece of paper just waiting for the gifted musicians to cover it with their own creations. The very lack of knowledge that she had deplored made her a perfect medium, ideal for their purposes.

The rather dismal facts of Rosemary's life added further authenticity to her story. Skeptics invariably accused her of secretly having had advanced musical training in her past and then lying about it. Kinder, more tactful skeptics suggested that she had had early training of an extensive nature but then had suffered amnesia and forgotten it. Both of these theories can and have been quickly dispelled by Rosemary's family doctor, who has known her since birth. Friends, relatives, and local authorities have verified that she has lived all her life in one residence and that her existence as a child, a wife, and finally as a widow has been one of financial deprivation. There simply was no piano training other than the most elementary kind, and this ended long before the compositions began.

"I've had to rise above so much in life that I suppose I was forced to develop tremendous will power," Rosemary conjectures. "It's an essential quality because the work can be so grueling. So much has gone wrong in my life that I've also acquired a kind of passivity. I just don't fight against things that are merely personal issues. I suppose this rather placid, docile nature does make it easier for me to receive them."

Some compensation for all her difficulties may have come from Rosemary's free-wheeling association with the composers, some of whom have become almost a part of her family.

"Ask Liszt, he'll know," Rosemary's daughter, Georgina, will implore when she is late for school and unable to find her boots.

"They are behind the piano where you left them," Liszt will remind her.

Once when things were particularly difficult for Rosemary financially, Liszt advised her to bet on a football pool. She won $25. Another time when funds were low and Christmas looming large on the horizon, he suggested that she try again. This time Rosemary's winnings were $125. "It was a kind of minor miracle," she says today, "and especially amazing since I have never made a practice of filling in football coupons. I've never done it since either. Those two experiences were special favors, gifts from the beyond at a time when I truly needed them. I wouldn't presume to try again."

Liszt has helped in other ways equally mundane. One afternoon Rosemary was about to fly to Dublin to appear on a television show when she discovered that she had mislaid her boarding pass. Already nervous, she frantically searched through her purse. "It's in your pocket," Liszt sighed. (It was, too.)

"Liszt just can't understand why I'm frightened of appearing before an audience," Rosemary admits. "Naturally a great artist and performer such as he was has a well-developed ego. Public appearances were food and drink to him in this life. They are sheer torture for me."

But Liszt can be very understanding about other matters. He frequently accompanies Rosemary to the supermarket and points out bargains. "No, not that bunch of bananas; there's a cheaper one over there," he once said, pointing. (He was quite right.) Liszt keeps track of the totals, too. More than once Rosemary has had to return items to the shelves when she's reached the check-out stand and found herself with more groceries than she has money to pay for. This never happens when Liszt goes along.

Liszt also helps the Brown children with their homework and once warned Rosemary in the morning that there would be three fires that day. Two minor ones so unnerved her that when a pan of cooking fat accidentally caught fire she completely panicked. "Put the pan in the sink," Liszt ordered. Rosemary hesitated, as the flames were high and she was afraid of burning her hands. "Go ahead, it won't harm you," he urged.

"I really doubt that I'd have had the courage to lift the flaming pan without his encouragement," she says, "but he was quite right. I wasn't hurt at all and the fire was quickly extinguished."

Chopin, too, has been a kind of household helper at times. One day he suddenly interrupted his dictating of a new composition and began gesturing wildly and chattering in French. Rosemary is hardly a linguist, but after meeting so many French-speaking spirits she has picked up a few phrases here and there. When she caught the words bath and water, she rushed upstairs and discovered that her daughter, Georgina, had left the water running in the bathtub and it was just about to overflow.

Each composer has a very distinct personality as he did in life. Liszt is very sensitive and once disappeared for several days when Rosemary mentally called him a "fusspot." (Mediums have very little privacy where spirits are involved.) Chopin is excitable and protective and enjoys wearing dramatic clothing, flaring capes and vibrant purple garments. Schubert is "lovable" and eager for Rosemary's opinion of his music after receiving it. "Do you really like that?" he'll ask hopefully. "Brahms is just the opposite. His manner is perfunctory," she says. "I'm here to receive his music and he appears not at all concerned with my opinion of it."

Rosemary finds Debussy the most original of her composer—a bit too original at times. Sometimes his kinky clothes and unconventional views make her a bit uncomfortable; but in her kindly, uncritical fashion, Rosemary easily makes allowances for the mannerisms and opinions that shock her. "Liszt says I'm inclined to be rather prim," she concedes. "Debussy is a very deep thinker, and aren't they always a bit unorthodox? Actually I don't think he was really as wild in this life as people say—bizarre clothes and sleeping with so many women and all. Anyway, nowadays that wouldn't be considered so terrible, now would it?

"It's the same with Liszt," she believes. "He is a very loving, outgoing person besides having been a terribly popular performer. He's like Rudolph Valentino or the Beatles. Some women simply could not stay away. What could a man do? I think many people just misunderstood his kindness. Of course today no one would think anything of the actions that seemed so shocking then."

Most contemporary musicians agree that it would be impossible for Rosemary or anyone else to have personally written all the music that she has received in so many different styles. A musical selection might be played in any given composer's style, but actually to compose in that style and in many others is a very difficult—if not impossible—thing.

Stewart Robb, an accomplished pianist and harpsichordist who holds a L.A.B., a performer's degree in music from the London Royal Academy and the London Royal College of Music, commented on Rosemary's abilities in an article in *Psychic Magazine.* "It is nearly impossible for the masters themselves to copy the style of another without their own style coming through," he writes.

"For example, Beethoven read, studied and played the scores of Haydn and Mozart, but even his first two symphonies—impossible without his predecessors—are pregnant with his own fire. And when Tchaikovsky transcribed for orchestra a set of piano variations on Mozart, quite literally one can still hear the Russian master all over the place, for his orchestration betrays him. Schumann, Chopin's friend, in his masterpiece *Carnival* included a gem called 'Chopin,' which is and is not Chopin. Or, if you will, it is Chopin heard through Schumann's mind.

"Another hypothesis submitted has been that Mrs. Brown produces these compositions through subconscious mystical powers, a telepathic force able to tune in on the minds of living musicians or even on the universe of music itself. If so, it is still a mystery how she produces her musical structures without part of herself coming through. And none of these compositions bear her style—whatever that might be—but each has the style of its respective composer.

"One Beethoven sonata has been called a poor thing— more like a Beethoven sketch for a sonata than a sonata itself. This may indeed be the case, but here again it does not necessarily invalidate the music and even the alleged source, since the most that can be said in the criticism is that the music is not the best Beethoven, not that it is unlike him.

"This, interestingly enough, has been one of the admissions of even the critical—the Beethoven sounds like early Beethoven, the Chopin like early Chopin, and so on. None say it is unlike the attributed composers."

Yet verification of Rosemary's music continues to pose many problems. If she receives information from her composers that is heretofore unknown, there is no way of checking it. If the information can be checked, then there is always someone to say that she read it somewhere—no matter how rare or obscure the source. She has been investigated and reinvestigated. Both *Life Magazine* and the BBC spent months checking into Rosemary's rather prosaic past. Then just prior to making her record, the Philips Recording Company asked if she would agree to being tested by Dr. W. H. C. Tenhaeff, director of the Institute of Parapsychology at the State University of Utrecht in Holland, and his team of experts.

The fact that these experts included an asylum psychiatrist did give Rosemary some pause. "Liszt had never said that it would be easy, but this was a bit much," she declared. But once more Rosemary gave in and at least had the consolation of being pronounced sane by the experts. The battery of tests to which she was subjected dispelled many other theories as well. She does not suffer from cryptomnesia (hidden memory) nor did the psychiatric and psychological testing reveal any mental aberrations.

"The results," Dr. Tenhaeff wrote, "showed that we have to deal with a woman of sound mental balance who is not in the least anxious to occupy the limelight."

The fact that Rosemary has allowed herself to be forced into a limelight position, where she is required not only to make personal appearances that are a miserable ordeal for such a shy, retiring personality, but must also face alone the derision and scorn of the skeptical and the verbal and even physical abuse of the ignorant is a true measure of her dedication to the composers' goal.

Though the approaches are slightly different, the ultimate goal is the same for all the musicians that she has "received." Rosemary was surprised to find that each has his own conception of God. Debussy regards Him as infinity. Liszt perceives Him as a spirit who permeates everything and is everything and yet is aware of individual thought and can receive prayers. Chopin sees Him as a holy spirit that will come through to all if we channel ourselves to accept Him.

When Rosemary expressed doubts that a kindly god could countenance such travesties of nature as Thalidamide babies, Liszt assured her that there was a divine purpose in such seeming tragedies. "All of us need to learn fortitude during our time on earth. Those who experience extreme suffering may have chosen this fate prior to birth in order to learn patience and courage," he said.

This philosophy is the basic reason for the manifestations of the composers, Rosemary believes. "They are anxious to show the world that they are still on the job and want to demonstrate that there is a continuity of personality. They feel that people would be much happier if they knew that life on earth is only a preliminary to a much more wonderful life after death," she says. "Once Liszt told me that life on our earth is very like a nursery school. No matter how wasted some lives may seem, there is always another chance to catch up."

He explains the process of reincarnation as putting out a fresh shoot on a tree or plant. Though humans may think of themselves as complete beings, only an aspect of each entity is actually manifested through the physical body and brain. The rest of the entity remains whole in spirit but is linked and one with the human body. When an entity is born again, he or she will have different parents, a different body, different brain, different background and ancestry— everything will be different. But a part of that central "tree" would be infused into the new person, just as a tree or plant puts out a new leaf. When the individual "dies," he or she is reunited with the original whole as the infusion returns to its origin.

"The identical person does not keep shuttling back

and forth to earth in the same body. We're much bigger than that," Rosemary now believes. "Supposing this central origin had a link with England," she suggests. "It might then put out another shoot to India. That soul could later appear as an Englishman or an Indian. It could be compared to an actor. He plays many parts but always remains essentially the same inside no matter how he may disguise himself outwardly.

"Chopin says the exact same flower would never blossom twice, but a plant would send out several other blossoms. The return to earth is a voluntary act and results from a desire to learn a lesson. If an individual is prejudiced against blacks or women, for instance, he will surely return as a black or a woman so that he can work through that feeling."

The ultimate universal revelation of this grand scheme is the motivation behind Rosemary's efforts and those of the composers. Though she has received some remuneration for her record, it is very small considering the all-consuming effort involved. The money has merely been enough to enable her to quit her job in the school cafeteria and devote her full-time efforts to taking spiritual dictation.

Liszt warned her from the very beginning that the task would not be an easy one. " 'You must be prepared to suffer,' he said and I certainly have," Rosemary admits. "The majority of people are kind. Even if they don't believe my music comes from dead composers, they'll be courteous, but there are others—I've had to ask the police to protect me and to hire a lawyer. Religious fanatics have actually attacked me and threatened my children. They called me a witch and said I was in league with the dead."

Rosemary's witchhood is questionable, but her league with the dead has produced more than 500 musical compositions. Most of them are piano pieces, but she is also in the process of receiving Beethoven's Tenth Symphony, a highly complicated orchestral work.

Rosemary's work of receiving and transcribing music

is an ongoing thing. While continuing to hear from her "regulars," she also feels the presence of others who seem to be waiting in the wings for their turn to come through. "They are all welcome," she says. "The only trouble will be finding the time for everything they want to convey."

Betty Bethards

The Making of a Mystic

The greatest fear of any individual possessing the power of precognition came true for Betty Bethards, a Northern California mystic whose teachings may have altered the lives of millions.

Precognition—the unexplained ability to foretell the future—was hardly new to Betty. For years her predictions had enlightened others who sought paranormal insights. Then suddenly, without warning, a terrible scene flashed before her eyes—the death of her own son.

This knowledge, agonizing in its clarity, was followed by a sense of total abandonment. The spirit forces that had revealed themselves again and again through her for the benefit of others now seemed unable or unwilling to save the one that *she* loved.

Could a mother feel anything but bitterness and anguish at learning that her firstborn son would soon die?

Betty Bethards

C.J. Marrow

For all her supernatural gifts, Betty Bethards was as helpless as any other mortal. There were no precautions that she could take to protect her son. He was en route to Vietnam.

Tragic, despairing weeks passed and then official word came that her boy had been killed by an exploding land mine. Betty's spirit guides continued in their unaccustomed silence, leaving her bereft. It appeared to the grieving mother that the discarnate forces present since her childhood had forsaken her at the very time she had most need of them.

Why did I have to go through this? she cried to a seeming void. Finally, Betty says today, she sobbed aloud, "Can't you even say you're sorry?"

A voice responded: "*We cry at birth, we rejoice at death. It is you who are the illusion, we who are the reality.*"

The message seemed cold, heartless, unacceptable. Understanding came three months later as the result of a dream. "I saw my son, Wayne, standing before me," she recalls. "Rushing forward, I threw my arms about him and said, 'Where have you been? I've been looking all over for you!'

" 'Reviewing my past,' he answered. How sensible, I remember thinking approvingly. But as we talked I began to feel extreme depression that my daughter, Pam, wasn't with us. We three had always been so close. I had them both before I was nineteen and we grew up together. We were like the three musketeers.

"As I awakened, I experienced an overwhelming sense of grief that my *daughter* was dead. It persisted as I got up and walked down the hall, still paining over her loss. Then it hit me. 'Hey, wait a minute! It isn't Pam that's dead, it's Wayne!'

"I realized the truth then" Betty explains, "to them *we're* dead! They feel sorrow for us rather than for themselves."

Though Betty's early background and religious training were highly conservative, she has come to accept the doctrine of reincarnation. It has brought a sense of purpose and resignation to her life. Wayne's job in this incarnation had been completed. It was time for him to move on, she now believes.

As a psychic healer and teacher who, in 1974, reached five million people through radio, television, and lectures, Betty feels confident that she is successfully fulfilling her own predestined tasks. The Inner Light Foundation, a nonprofit organization comprising more than 1200 members, was formed spontaneously by volunteers eager to support Betty's doctrine of selfhelp, healing, and psychic awareness through meditation. As a result of the foundation's volunteer efforts in dispensing information, more than 500,000 people have attended free meditation groups in the state of California, with new groups springing up all across the nation.

Betty believes that she chose to assume this task before incarnating and is anxious to achieve her potential in this lifetime. She does *not* wish to live again. Sometimes the going gets rough, she admits. "If I knew how to get in touch with God, I'd resign," she often jokes. "But what good would it do? I'd only have to come back and start all over."

Betty Bethards the individual is one thing. The spirit guides who speak through her "channel" are something else.

"Don't confuse us," she often urges.

Anyone who accepts Webster's definition of a mystic as one "belonging to secret rites, beyond human comprehension, mysterious or enigmatic," reckons without Betty. This popular concept calls to mind an emaciated ascetic, living monastically in a cave on a diet of nuts and berries.

An avowed Pepsi-Cola addict and chain smoker, Betty does not fit the picture. She has a full womanly figure, resides with her third husband in a tract house, and enjoys bridge, bowling, and jigsaw puzzles. Betty's manner is direct and unpretentious, her vocabulary decidedly earthy. She seemingly differs from the lady next door only in her great candor and courage, her willingness to take emotional risks, to defy convention when necessary to fulfill inner needs.

Despite her psychic abilities, Betty is almost aggressively natural in her actions and attitudes. "No one will ever succeed in making a high priestess out of me," she maintains.

"That trip is a real bummer for everyone concerned. Nobody grows by leaning on someone else, yet everybody seems to be seeking a saint to direct them. Left to their own devices, they'll find a candidate and begin erecting a pedestal to place her on. I can't allow that or the whole idea of encouraging each individual to seek his or her own spiritual truths through personal meditation will be ruined. I put a stop to this guru business before it can get started by laying out all my frailties to everyone who cares to listen—on the radio, on television, and from the lecture platform. No one will ever do an exposé on me because I've said it all myself. I keep pounding away at the fact that I've got needs and emotions of my own to deal with just like anyone else. I'm *very* human."

Betty may be human but many of her closest friends are not.

Believing herself to be following a divine plan, Betty is not surprised to have encountered many helper spirits along the way. "I was set up for everything that happened to me," she believes. "No matter how strange it seemed at the time, there was always a reason."

It began at age two when Betty first became aware of "Helen," an entity that only she could see. "My family laughed at me because I would set my tea table for two and often talked aloud to Helen," Betty recalls. "I refused to eat dinner unless she was with me and wouldn't go to bed without her. It was humiliating to be ridiculed, but at the same time I *knew* that Helen was real and that her presence was essential to me."

The secret friend is not an unusual phenomenon, she believes. All only children or quiet, sensitive children will have a special friend that only they can see. A creative outlet must be established in such children, for imagination is their bridge to the world.

Betty is certain that Helen was sent to her at birth in order to stimulate her own creativity and imagination as well as the intuitive instinct that would ultimately lead her into the psychic world. "Though I have two sisters, they are so much older that I was raised as an only child," she explains. "It follows that Helen, a dear friend from another lifetime, was sent to watch over me and to foster my growth in a way that no human playmate ever could."

Betty's life has been an essentially lonely one—something she perceives as an inevitable part of the path that she was intended to follow. Her father was fifty at the time of her birth. A baby born at the height of the depression was hardly a boon to a man who had just lost his job.

It's likely that Dad would have ignored me anyway," Betty feels. "He was a serious, cigar-smoking man who regarded women as beings incapable of intelligence. It was many, many years before he came to realize that I might have an idea or two worth his consideration. Inevitably our relationship has been a kind of learning process for us both."

The imminent arrival of Betty coupled with the loss of work made it necessary for her parents to leave their home in Tucson, Arizona, and go to live with in-laws in Greensberg, Indiana. There Betty was born on September 23, 1933. Though they remained in Greensberg only a few months, Betty believes that her birthplace has mystical significance. It would later play an important part in her life.

Once reemployed in Tucson, Betty's father put in long hours as a railroad brakeman. Very little time was spent with his daughter.

Threats of hell and hopes of paradise heavily flavored the girl's first twelve years—with a strong accent on the former. Betty's mother was a strict Baptist, whose entire life centered about the church. Trotting obediently at her mother's heels, Betty's days were a somber round of Sunday school, prayer meetings, missionary meetings, sewing circles, Ladies' Aid, and Bible School. There was little contact with other children and no awareness of alternative lifestyles.

"I didn't know what a normal social life was," she says today. "Not only did my parents not drink, but they didn't even know anyone who did!

"Adolescence was especially difficult. I went from playing with dolls at twelve to boys at thirteen. The worst of it was that I developed so fast. I had forty-inch breasts by the time I was fifteen.

"Every boy in town was chasing me. I'd missed the normal companionship that most young girls have and simply did not know how to cope with my sudden popularity. Mother hadn't married until she was twenty-eight and that worried her. She was afraid that I might be a wallflower, too. She shoved me out but never told me *anything*. The first time I was kissed—at thirteen—I was convinced that I was pregnant. I must have sobbed uncontrollably for an hour. I was frightened and ashamed, yet confused by my natural response to affection—I'd had so little. The poor boy just wouldn't accept that anyone could be so naive. He kept reassuring me that I was all right, but I didn't know what to believe. Mother was thrilled that I was dating but refused even to recognize the existence of sex. *Good* people didn't talk about such things. My father didn't talk to me about *anything*, I certainly couldn't ask him. My church activities had kept me from forming friendships with other girls and there wasn't anyone in the church itself that I could speak with about my problems."

Not surprisingly Betty became pregnant at sixteen as a

result of her first sexual experience. Appalling as the event
seemed at the time, she feels that it was meant to be.
"Maybe the ensuing marriage wasn't made in heaven, but
the baby, Wayne, surely was," she says. "He and I were
always close and the little girl that I had two years later—
my only daughter—was very much a wanted child. Pam
was the only one of my four children to be 'planned' and I
began praying that she would be a girl two months before
her conception."

Betty feels that the six years immediately following
the marriage were given her as a kind of grace period, an
opportunity to experience a normal existence. Though
once again the dominant man in her life chose to isolate
himself through his work and unwillingness to communicate, Betty found great solace in her children. This
period of relative tranquillity was to end with dramatic
suddenness.

One morning while washing dishes, Betty became
aware of the presence of Jerry, a close friend who had died
the week before. She stood literally frozen at the sink, her
hands clenched about a soapy dish, as she stared at the
apparaition floating beside her. "He looked as he had
always looked except that he was suspended a few inches
off the floor," she says.

"I'm more alive than you are," Jerry reassured her.
Betty merely shook her head in bewilderment, shocked to
the very core of her being. As every Baptist knows, dead
people are put into the ground and docilely remain there
until Judgment Day.

Jerry obviously refused to recognize this fundamentalist axiom. Communicating with Betty through telepathy,
he explained that he had come to her for help because she
had the ability to "receive." It was essential that she
communicate some important information to Rose, his
wife. Calmly and precisely, he then issued specific instructions for the settling of his estate.

" 'No one but Jerry could have had that information,'

Rose said, when I relayed it to her," Betty explains today.

This corroboration was even more alarming than the original ghostly experience for Betty, who was anxiously attempting to explain away the episode in her own mind as some kind of bad dream. After settling his earthly financial problems, Jerry had prophesied that she would die at thirty-two.

"He just kind of faded away, leaving me with a whole new concept of death to deal with along with the knowledge that I wasn't going to be around very long to enjoy life. How would you feel if you were told that only ten years remained to you?" she asks. "I thought of my children. It was so sad to think that I wouldn't see them grown. I thought of all the things I enjoyed doing and all the things I wanted to do. I thought of the great unknown void that awaited me and I was absolutely terrified."

Betty now believes that this supernatural encounter, with its subsequent fear and challenge to her religious indoctrination, was all a part of the same plan that has governed her life since before birth. "My very deep friendship with Rose and Jerry wouldn't have developed if my marriage hadn't been an essentially lonely one. My husband's work left me alone so much that they literally adopted my babies and me into their own family," she explains.

"Jerry's death was meant to jolt me, to set me thinking and questioning the beliefs that I'd taken for granted. Obviously someone had a purpose in mind for me. They were saying, in effect: 'Hey, kid, you may think you know it all—but you don't.'"

Looking back over the events surrounding Jerry's death, Betty recalled the overwhelming urge she had felt, the insistent need to visit him at the hospital. Defying her angry husband, she had rushed out of the house in the midst of preparing dinner. "Don't you dare leave me with these unfed kids!" he'd yelled, attempting to grab the car keys from her.

"I locked myself in the car and drove away with him

still pounding on the window," she says. "You really can't imagine the courage that took! My husband was a very strong, domineering man with old country ideas about a woman's place. If I attempted to go anywhere when he was home, he'd knock me off the side of the wall. I knew what I was risking, but that all-consuming pressure to go to Jerry was too heavy to ignore. "Unfortunately after speeding to the hospital, I arrived just as Jerry died. I was with Rose when she received the sad news, but never saw Jerry as a 'live human' again."

Then Betty began to remember the funeral experience itself. Having never seen a corpse before, she was apprehensive and dreaded going to the funeral home. Still she felt that as Rose's closest friend it would be up to her to offer strength and support. Hoping to fortify herself for the ordeal, Betty went to the mortuary early to view the body before the other mourners arrived. After timidly peering into the casket, she drew back in surprise.

"That's not Jerry," she recalls thinking, "that's an empty shell. No longer afraid, I found myself looking around the room for him. I didn't remember these things when Jerry suddenly appeared in my kitchen but I thought of them afterward and I realize now that they subtly prepared me for what was to follow."

Betty tried to block these experiences from her mind. "I didn't want to see things that I couldn't understand. It was too confusing," she says today. "Then the dreams started. They were even more frightening, strange predictions of things that I couldn't possibly know. Often accidents and other tragedies were involved," she remembers. "Friends began saying, 'Do me a favor and don't dream about me tonight.' It wasn't funny. It was terrible."

During this period Betty was experiencing tragedies of her own. As the emotional estrangement from her husband became more and more unbearable, she was driven by some inner, unexplainable need to take a mysterious journey.

Leaving her children with relatives, she rode hundreds of miles by bus to Greensberg, Indiana, the place of her birth twenty-four years before. "No one in the family lived there any longer. I didn't know a soul, yet somehow I felt that it was absolutely necessary that I go," she explains, still clearly bewildered by the event.

Betty got off the bus and, without realizing how or why, walked straight to the town graveyard. As she paused, looking down at her brother's grave—a child who had died *before* her own birth—it became clearly apparent that her marriage of eight years must end. She turned, walked back to the depot, and boarded the bus for home. Betty's total time in Greensberg was an hour and a half. Yet she was certain that the purpose of her long wearisome trip had been fulfilled.

Years later Betty learned that twice in the lives of her two older sisters they also had visited the Greensberg graveyard. "These trips had been quite unknown to each other or to me," she says. "Somehow this little town has filled a mystic need in all of our lives."

Betty was divorced, ultimately remarried, and had two more children. Unfortunately Chris Bethards, Betty's second husband, was yet another man who escaped personal communication with her through absorption in his work. Once again there was an aching void to fill.

Betty was now thirty-two. Another major crossroad loomed ahead. One night she awakened suddenly to find herself hovering over the bed about two feet above her actual physical body. "You're going to have pneumonia," a voice warned. "Get a doctor."

Panic-stricken, she awakened her husband. "I was floating above my body," she sobbed.

"That's okay, honey," he murmured sleepily. "You'll be all right in the morning."

The next day Betty was *not* all right and insisted that she be taken to a physician. The doctor seemed unconcerned by her fever, merely advising that she go home and take an aspirin. In the two weeks that followed, she grew steadily weaker while her temperature rose to 104.

"I was confused and frightened," she remembers. "Doctors are supposed to know everything, but there I was getting worse and worse. Then one afternoon as I lay on the couch I somehow seemed to move out of myself. There I was standing twenty feet across the room staring at my body—a body that I now realized was only a shell. My mind, my personality, what I knew as 'Betty,' was sympathetically viewing the body. 'Gee, she's sick,' I can recall thinking. I didn't want to go back to that body."

Betty's reverie was broken by a voice. "You don't have to go back," it informed her. "But this is death if you choose to stay."

She looked in wonderment at her new self. "I had a body which appeared the same and was wearing the same clothes, but it was raised a few feet off the floor. I wasn't frightened at all. In fact, it's really impossible to describe the great ecstasy that I experienced in those minutes. I'd never known such ultimate peace. One thing I knew for certain, I didn't want to go back to that old Betty lying on the couch. And I wouldn't have returned to her, but then I thought of my children—particularly my thirteen-month-old baby. The others could make it, but not the little one. He was still so young."

Betty says that she returned to her body after a parting warning from the voice who foretold that there would be no choice unless she took an antibiotic within twenty-four hours. After being rushed to the doctor's office, Betty found that her regular physician was away. In his absence, she was treated by his partner. The man, appalled by his associate's presumably casual approach, X-rayed Betty and diagnosed her case as pneumonia. He prescribed an antibiotic that broke her fever within hours.

The experience put an end forever to Betty's concern for her own life. She could understand at last how Jerry had been able to come to her ten years before. Could he have known then that she would have a choice of life, she pondered, or did he perceive her death at thirty-two as inevitable? Surely her own inclination had been to die.

"It was only the baby that stopped me," she says, "but certainly that too was part of a plan devised in the other world. The baby was a miraculous conception if there ever was one. He was conceived the day after my period ended and that just isn't supposed to happen. My marriage was falling apart. Discovering that I was pregnant held it together. It was just one more setup—God's way of saying, 'Not so fast there! You're not ready for that yet.' We might *think* that we direct our own lives, but forget it! There's an over-all plan that can change our own timetable entirely."

The months that followed this dramatic experience were marked by intense personal struggle and self-doubt. Betty began to hear voices and to feel herself in touch with a passing parade of spirits who seemed to hover about her. Beginning at last to doubt her own sanity, she sought the advice of doctors and ministers.

At last her own clergyman counseled, "As long as what you're being told is good, there seems to be no harm in continuing. Pray for guidance and ask God to help you to understand what is happening."

There were long agonizing nights of prayer, sometimes for four and five hours at a stretch. Betty's spiritual experiences intrigued her husband, Chris, who was an engineer with no religious background or—until then—interest in the supernatural. Chris' concern for her and his interest in what was happening brought them closer, as well as providing the moral support Betty desperately needed to continue.

"I simply could not have done it without him," she states flatly. "At one point I was so confused and frightened by the whole thing that I felt totally unable to persevere. 'I quit!' I told him at last, adding in the hope of convincing us both, 'it's probably just my imagination anyway.'

" 'That's okay, dear,' he replied, gently, reassuringly, 'you stop if you feel that you must. But I'm not going to stop trying to listen for the answers. I've got to go on.'

" 'How can he go on?' I remember thinking. 'He doesn't hear or see anything; how can he possibly continue without me?' It seemed somehow that I had to go on for his sake. His faith seemed to be growing all the time and with it was a sense of obligation on my part not to let him down."

Betty prayed for four days, asking that she be told once and for all what was going on and how to understand the variety of voices, the conflicting instructions and unexplainable visions that made her life a continuing nightmare. "I've got to have a sign that this isn't just in my head or I'll shut the door on you!" she warned the forces that plagued her. At the same time Betty wondered if she had the power to make good her threat.

At the end of four days of prayerful meditation, Chris joined her and they continued to pray in silence together. Then, Betty claims, there was a sudden rush of energy into the room and she felt herself levitated, raised into the air.

The experience made a believer of Chris. Betty's reaction was, "Oh God, They're going to drop me on my nose!"

"They" didn't. Having demanded a sign, she had been given one. Slowly Betty floated down to earth—gently landing on her feet.

A few days later the spirit guide, Uvalla, appeared and introduced himself as Betty's teacher from a former Peruvian incarnation. "I knew him right away," she says, "we had an instant rapport that could only have been gained through lifetimes of mutual trust and effort. He was exactly what I needed, for I was still very frightened and uncertain about what was happening. But when Uvalla merged with me, I knew his soul. I had the sense of knowing his every feeling, his every thought. I knew that he was kind, gentle, and loving. I was certain that he would never, never hurt me. That confidence was exactly what I needed the first year and a half. It gave me the courage to go on. I'm much stronger now, but I know that Uvalla is still standing guard. He's my doorkeeper and would never allow anyone or anything through who would endanger me."

Betty says that Uvalla taught her a means of controlling her psychic and spiritual development and a simple meditation technique which she has since passed on to thousands. As Betty's psychic gifts ripened under Uvalla's tutelage, she became clairvoyant, clairaudient, and clairsentient. This means that she can see, hear, and sense events often before they happen. She has also developed a psychic energy flow that has healed many who were physically or emotionally ill.

Dr. William Tiller, who was chairman of the Department of Sciences at Stanford University from 1966 to 1971 and is now a government consultant in the fields of metallurgy and solid-state physics, has had an opportunity to study Betty's gifts firsthand.

While investigating acupuncture treatments in Russia, Tiller observed that when scientists measured the same acupuncture points on both the right and left sides of the body they got a certain degree of resistance.

"If they then turned the electrodes around and measured in the reverse direction, the scientists found the same degree of resistance—if the individual was healthy," Tiller explained. "If he was not, there was a distinct difference in resistance in proportion to the degree of the disease."

Several Russian scientists did another experiment that Dr. Tiller later duplicated with Betty. A healer was used to project energy to a sick person whose circuits had been established by the electrodes as unbalanced. Six points were measured on both the patient and the healer before the experiment began. The patient showed an imbalance; the healer did not.

"After the projection of healing energy, the ill person was measured again," he says. "The patient's *differential* resistance had *decreased* which meant that he was getting healthier. The healer's differential resistance had *in-*

creased, indicating that he had partially unbalanced his own circuits in order to help balance the patient's."

Dr. Tiller's own experiments with Betty were even more dramatic. "I had an acupuncture measuring device and my wife, Jean, was suffering from an abdominal problem, a deficient pancreas condition," he explained.

"The acupuncture pressure points for my wife's abdomen happened to be on the side of the knees. So I applied the electrodes, measuring from left to right and from right to left and got a difference in resistance of about twenty per cent. Next I measured Betty and found no difference. We did not use acupuncture needles. Instead Betty projected healing energy into the acupuncture points at the knees with her hands. The resistance changed in both of them. But there was still a difference. So I said, 'Okay, just put the energy in one knee.' This she did, but the difference *increased* because I'd picked the wrong knee!

"Uvalla, communicating through Betty, said that it wasn't necessary to put this kind of energy into the knees. Instead, he instructed that she put it into the back of Jean's neck. He explained that the body had its own individual intelligence in terms of knowing where best to use this kind of healing energy. Betty obediently projected her energy into the back of Jean's neck. I measured the resistance points and found that they had changed. I then measured them daily for about a week and a half. The resistance at these places had doubled in magnitude, which meant that the health condition had gone up. Then finally there was no longer any differential resistance—and the abdominal condition was gone! Unlike the Russian healers, Betty suffered no loss to her own energies."

Betty believes that this healing was made possible because of her ability to channel energy. "What has happened from all these years of meditation is that I'm like a receiving station," she says. "The higher my frequency, the more I can tune in; so of course I strive through daily meditation to develop a higher and higher channel."

She feels personally removed from the information channeled in this manner. "I hear me talking, giving out information, but it's as if I am able to suspend the workings of my conscious mind so that another dimension is able to function," she explains.

Working with doctors and psychiatrists, Betty has had a therapeutic effect upon patients in Napa and Sonoma hospitals in California. "Most of us would like to tune in to the psychic world in order to gain peace and spiritual insights," she says, "but in mental hospitals there are many who suffer terribly because they can't tune out.

"Once while visiting an ill friend who had asked me for help—a patient in the mental ward of the San Francisco Presidio—I happened to notice another patient who was standing next to me at the Coke machine. Without his saying a word, I knew exactly what was happening in his head. It was so tragic that I reached out and took his hand and lead him to some chairs where we both sat down. 'I know that you're going to be released in a few days,' I said to him. No one had told me and I'd never seen the man before in my life, but I knew it. Then I said, 'I feel that you're terribly unhappy and plan to commit suicide as soon as you're out of here. *Don't!'*

"The man burst into tears. When he could finally control his sobs, he said: 'I even had my funeral planned.' I told him about meditation and the difference it's made in my life and countless others. I promised to help him and insisted that he call me as soon as he was out. That was in 1971. We're still in touch with one another. Meditation is a part of his daily life and he's a happy, well-adjusted individual.

"But that was just one sick frightened soul. There are so many in mental institutions and it's so hard to reach them through conventional methods. Just because most people don't hear the same voices or see the same visions as the schizophrenic doesn't mean that they don't exist. I show them how to close down, to shut out the voices that distract them. It's been an effective alternative to shock treatments."

An Oakland psychiatrist, Dr. Ernest Pecci, director of the Fisher-Hoffman Institute, says that Betty does this by merely putting her hand on the patient's shoulders. In this way she is able to raise the patient's energy level, thus depleting the forces tormenting him.

"Of course," he clarifies, "Betty has the power; but, in the final analysis, it is the patient who must assume responsibility for the ultimate healing. Betty's energy flow can give tremendous relief, but it is only temporary if the mentally ill individual doesn't really want to be well. Betty's most important contribution is in stimulating the will to be well within the patient. Her successes in this area have been phenomenal."

Dr. Pecci has often observed Betty's channel at work and has himself referred patients to her. "I believe that people are essentially ill because they want to be. Insights provided by Betty's channels, her psychic energies, and the meditation techniques that she teaches have had a positive effect upon many, many lives."

He cites the case of a woman diagnosed as having severe stomach cancer. "It's a condition called linus plasticous," he explains. "Doctors operated, determined conclusively that the condition was hopeless, and immediately sewed her back up. Death was only days away, they advised regretfully. The patient visited Betty and experienced an immediate remission. 'I have never felt so well or so happy in my entire life,' she told me many times in the months that followed. I saw her life take on new meaning and purpose. She discovered great strengths within herself that had seemingly been nonexistent before. She was able to make peace within her family—something that had previously been inconceivable. Two years later the patient did die; but it was as though she herself had picked the time. There was no fear or sadness. In their place I saw only a great tranquillity and satisfaction. She seemed to feel that her purpose in life and been fulfilled and was ready to move on."

There is no question in Dr. Pecci's mind that Betty has access to a high channel that can inform as well as heal. "Many times we've discussed problems that have arisen in my treating of emotionally disturbed patients," he says. "Betty has often used her channel to check out my diagnoses. I remember one instance in particular. It involved a patient that I sensed must go her own way without me. I felt that I could no longer help her and might in fact restrict her recovery. When I discussed my conclusions with the patient, she became highly upset and threatened suicide. 'Don't leave me,' she begged frantically.

"It was an extremely difficult decision for me to make. Betty's channel tuned in to the emotional situation. 'The patient should be on her own,' it verified. 'You need have no fear of suicide. She will be stronger for going it alone and will progress much faster.' " Later events confirmed that Dr. Pecci was correct in dismissing the patient.

"Many mediums confuse themselves with their channels," Dr. Pecci points out. "The danger in this is that they are inclined to go off on ego trips and start giving orders. That's not Betty's way. She is a simple, unassuming person, but her astral level is very high and this she uses to tune into the highest level of consciousness within the individual involved."

Betty believes that the basic message channeled through her again and again since first making contact with Uvalla in 1966 is one of personal responsibility. "We are all accountable for our every thought, our every word, our every action," she says. "Our purpose here on earth is to grow in understanding, in knowledge, and in love. None of us can do it all in a single lifetime so we are given many opportunities from which to unfold spiritually.

"Many times people will come up to me and say, 'Since belonging to one of your meditation groups, my whole life has changed for the better. I can't thank you enough.' I try to set them straight by reminding, 'Don't thank me. I must have loused you up sometime before. If you feel better, it means that I've just been setting the record straight.' They still don't realize how grateful *I* am to be on the right track myself."

Betty has recollections of a former lifetime on the lost continent of Atlantis. This memory, she believes, was revealed to her for a reason. "All this 'who you were before' stuff is kind of hokey," she feels. "It's only relevant if it affects what you are doing now. That's where the real lesson lies.

"My previous incarnation was revealed to me because of my intense concern over Vietnam following my son's death. It seemed that all the boys dying there were my own children. All my energies were caught up in anger and frustration. I could think of nothing but my tremendous desire to bring them all home. Then one night, while meditating, a voice said: 'You've done this before in Atlantis. You had the same gifts there and were a teacher of meditation; then you gave it up in useless protest against the treatment of prisoners. Now you have a choice. You can abandon yourself to useless torment regarding Vietnam which will do no good or you can fulfill your potential. Through meditation you are teaching people to open their eyes to prejudice, famine, ecology, even war itself, for you are teaching people to care. If you forsake that as you did in Atlantis, it will cost you another incarnation and possibly 1200 years to ultimately reach the same point.' This message really pulled me up short for I began to remember strange and horrifying experiences that related to me in another body at another time and place. There was simply no doubt in my mind that my job in this lifetime is strictly to be a teacher of meditation."

There's really nothing new about meditation, Betty is quick to point out. "People have been doing it for thousands of years," she says, "but in the Western world many of us tend to think of it as vague and mysterious or possibly just something for kooks or kids. When people see me doing it, they realize that there's a message for everyone on every level of consciousness and experience."

Explaining meditation in its simplest terms, Betty calls it a means of going within, of discovering oneself. It is not a religion; yet it can enrich any faith. It offers no magic answer to life's problems and is not an escape from life. It is not an end in itself, but rather a beginning.

"On one level meditation can develop inner peace and serenity," she explains. "It can free the individual from frustrations and anxieties. It can help to overcome hostilities and to find clearer directions in life. On a deeper level it can bring one in touch with powerful unseen energies within the universe. Healing abilities may ultimately manifest themselves along with psychic insights. But most important," Betty stresses again and again, "is an inner knowing, a receptiveness to the deeper meaning of one's own existence."

Betty's meditation technique is simple enough for anyone to understand and easily adaptable to the most active lifestyle. The requirements are merely a quiet place to be alone and twenty minutes a day. Before beginning, she advises that a few relaxing moments be spent reading something inspirational, such as poetry or religious writings or listening to uplifting music. Then the meditator is to visualize himself surrounded by a protective bubble of white light. (This same thought should close the session.)

After selecting a comfortable sitting position in which the spine is straight and the feet flat on the floor, Betty suggests that the hands be folded or placed gently together with palms and fingertips touching. The eyes may be either open or closed. Attention should be focused on one word, or a symbol, a picture, or feeling, but thought should be directed only toward *one* thing during the concentration period and this should be something personally suggestive of beauty, joy, love and peace.

"Hold this image to the best of your ability for a full

ten minutes," she insists, "and whenever your mind wanders, gently draw it back and continue. This process brings about an interaction of the physical, the mental, and the spiritual-building energy while promoting harmonious vibrations.

"After ten minutes of concentration—or when it feels right—just turn the hands over, palms up, and let them rest gently on your lap. Release your mind from its controlled attention and permit thoughts to flow. You will now be in a state of 'passive awareness.' Imagine yourself watching a motion picture, letting it progress without attempting to hold on to any one object or idea."

Betty believes that this free-flowing receptiveness is a time of listening and learning. "The input may appear in pictures or images," she suggests, "or for others it may take the form of feelings or even voices. New ideas could just seem to 'pop in' or you may sense increased energy. Whatever happens, accept it as your deeper, inner self developing into conscious awareness."

As a result of many years of such meditation, Betty's belief in reincarnation and karma—the inevitable law of cause and effect—has developed. "Karma simply means you will harvest exactly what you have planted," she explains. "It is the principle of individual responsibility. You control your own destiny by your thoughts, words, and deeds. The Western world is familiar with the idea, though not linked with the concept of reincarnation, through the words of St. Paul: 'Whatsoever a man soweth, that shall he also reap.'

"The very word, 'karma,' means action. It's a kind of action and reaction that applies to nations and races as well as individuals. This process of universal education works with the inevitability of any natural law. The current ecological crisis is one example, war is another. Until millions stop attributing these disasters to chance they will continue to perpetuate, as will our own personal disasters —disease, poverty, alienation of loved ones. These things don't just happen. They are a direct result of past actions. Memory is largely erased at birth, but the spiritually evolved person can often see or sense prior lifetimes. We don't have to keep making the same mistakes, only to receive the same legacy of bitterness and anguish."

Some psychics, Betty included, believe they can see the previous lifetimes of others. But more important, she feels, *everyone* can *know* that he or she personally chose the circumstances of the present life—parents, race, sex, nationality, economic condition, appearance, etc. What we as individuals experience is what we have *chosen* to experience. The purpose of it all is to grow, to develop spiritual understanding and the ability to love unselfishly.

Betty believes that every family has been together in previous incarnations. "You never incarnate into a new family; you never marry a man or become involved in any close relationship with someone that you have not been close to before," she insists.

She is certain that all who are dear to her in this life played important roles in previous incarnations. "My father and first two husbands avoided closeness with me to a marked degree, and yet in each relationship I in some way played a mother-teacher part. I know that I somehow deserted them in the past. In this life, I've had to face up to that karma. While terribly painful at times, it has taught me to accept loneliness and to think and act for myself. I hope that I've discharged my debts to them all by being honest and sincere in my dealings. I've certainly tried to.

"I am certain that I was once married to Wayne, my oldest son who died. I believe my twelve-year-old boy was once my father—never doubted it for a minute from the day he was born. My twenty-two-year-old daughter was surely my mother at one time or another. I gave up fighting her when she was thirteen. I said, 'Pam, I can't do it. You're not going to allow me to do it, so you be the mother.' She still is. In fact, Pam is now my secretary and kind of runs the show."

In the case of an adopted child, Betty's channels have revealed that the soul of the unborn "walks" with its adoptive parents for two years prior to its conception by the natural parents. "There is a clarity on the other side that we don't possess," she explains. "They know where the entity is going to be after birth and they also know if the child will be aborted."

An abortion, too, can be according to a divine plan, Betty believes. "There's always a reason for conception," she says. "Perhaps the entity may need only two months in the human world to fulfill some karmic need. If the mother does not want to bring that child to term, she shouldn't. If no one outside of herself and the entity inside her are affected by the abortion and the prospective mother feels strongly about not having the child—she shouldn't have it. On the other hand, if there is a sense of guilt involved, this may be a karmic warning not to abort."

The philosophy channeled to Betty—unlike her early religious instruction—is essentially one of great tolerance and compassion for human needs. "They understand the bed thing because they realize that it's a simple yearning for love and affection," she believes. "A lot of men who are going out on their wives are just saying 'tell me I'm masculine.' They're trying desperately to feed their starving egos. The woman who commits adultery is merely seeking warmth and affection. She's pleading, 'tell me I'm loved.'

"No one is going to judge us for wanting love. That's what life is all about. God isn't up there saying, 'If you slept with fifty people, we're going to condemn you' any more than He would condemn homosexuality. Homosexual or heterosexual—what difference does it make? It's all love and love is pure.

"Those aren't the kind of laws that we're judged by. Anybody who has been meditating for three years or more is going to perceive the karmic laws of cause and effect. It's easier to avoid mistakes because you see a pattern laid out before you. After a time it becomes apparent that every trauma is a turning point. Painful as it may be, it's still growth. Whatever lessons we have chosen to learn before birth are certain to be drawn to us."

As a result of Betty's own inner struggles, her long hours of meditation and prayers, she has developed a tremendous energy flow. There is no question that people attending her lectures or even listening to her on the radio or watching her on television can feel this force. On a person-to-person level, it feels like an energy current that reacts to the body like an electrical charge.

"People are drawn to that energy and it can be a tremendous force for good," she says. "It is easy for me to get a crowd centered into a collective force within twenty minutes. But I must also accept the responsibility for the power emanating through me. It would be easy to go off on an ego trip, but I know that if people lean on me or anyone else for their answers, they'll only have to come back and go through it all again. Decision making must be up to the individual. I say again and again, 'Don't go to psychics. Meditate. Get answers from your own light. Seek solutions from your dreams. If the symbolism confuses you, work on it.' The whole key is in getting enough of an aura built up to buffer other people's negativity and at the same time give yourself clarity to read what's being channeled to you."

Meditating makes it easier to recognize when one is on the right track. "On your own, you could become hurt or frustrated, thinking that you are being blocked from something that seems really important. Meditation will help you to know when it's time to divert your energies temporarily to another direction. On the other hand, when you see those doors open—you must go through no matter how scary it may seem at the time."

Betty came to such a turning point in her own life when a drug addict, AWOL from the Army, was literally dumped on her doorstep with a note pinned to his shirt. It read, "Dear Betty, have a Greg."

Greg, the young soldier abandoned in this callous manner by former friends who had helped him to squander his inheritance and then had grown bored with his company, had suffered a series of personal tragedies. His mother had died the day he was ordered to Saigon. While he was serving in Vietnam, his sweetheart was blown up by a land mine. Working as a medic, he saw a continual stream of dead and dying friends for whom he could do nothing. As the pressure mounted, he resorted to drugs and finally to escape from the military. Betty invited the frightened young man into her home, taught him effective meditation techniques, and was ultimately able to persuade him to turn himself in. After Greg had served his sentence, he returned to the Bethards' home.

Soon it was painfully apparent to Betty and to Greg that they were deeply in love. "This realization was a shattering experience for me," Betty says today. "I thought, 'My, God, what have you laid on me!" The whole situation seemed impossible, almost incomprehensible. A divorce would be damning enough for the head of a philosophical foundation dedicated to promoting inner peace. I thought of myself as someone whose job it was to set a kind of example. The mere idea of marrying a man fifteen years younger than myself seemed beyond belief. If Wayne had lived, they would have been almost the same age!

"I kept meditating, pleading for guidance, but all the while I was certain that I already knew the answer. I've always prayed to the forces to block me right away if they perceive me drifting off into the wrong direction. They always do, like the Atlantis thing. If I'm blowing it, they will lay it out for me so beautifully. It's been a great time saver. *That's* what I expected—a warning of some kind, maybe a spiritual spanking."

What Betty got was something entirely different. After weeks of prayer and meditation, a voice literally cried out in the night: *"Dare to be you."*

"I thought a long time about that one," Betty admits.

"Finally I accepted the message for what it was—another setup. Greg, too, was a part of the divine plan. Sometimes it takes a lot of guts to be yourself, but that's what they were telling me to do. It had been foolish of me to worry about the Inner Light Foundation. It wasn't *my* foundation! It had always belonged to God. I'd never asked for it. I never wanted the responsibility. It just happened around me because that was the way it was all meant to happen. After pushing and priming me all these years, the forces simply would not allow their efforts to be jeopardized. *They* had brought Greg into my life. Who was I to question their planning?

"Chris was wonderfully understanding. We both knew that we had gone as far as we could together. He continued to work for the foundation and within a year had married a group meditation leader. It's all been for the best and we both know it. But my marriage to Chris was only one obstacle. The idea of marrying Greg was very scary. The age thing frightened me and I worried, too, about his emotional problems. Could I cope with it all?"

Betty says that the answers came to her in yet another mystical vision. Once again she was awakened in the middle of the night. This time she awoke to find an oriental man bathed in a beautiful golden light standing by her bed. "Guidance comes from many sources both in and out of the body," he reminded her, "but ultimately you must make your own decisions and perceive your own destiny."

Betty interpreted his words as meaning that it was time for her to stop hesitating and get on with her life. "I thought, 'Gosh, that's beautiful. I'd better get up and write it down. Nothing like that would ever come out of *my* head.' I got up, got a pencil, paper, candy bar, glass of milk, and a cigarette and got back into bed. Then suddenly I realized that he hadn't faded away at all. He was still there watching me! Can you imagine how wonderful it was to have this marvelous guru right there? I could ask him any question that I'd ever wanted to know! I guess what I really wanted most was help and encouragement with Greg. I pleaded, 'Can't you shape him up for me?'

"The man replied, 'If you cannot live by that which you preach, you should not preach it. You tell others not to judge their fellow men and yet you with the very one that you love best are critical and judgmental. Worry about your own weaknesses and frailties for you will be judged for them when you cross over just as Greg will be judged for his.' "

Betty has found the subsequent marriage a highly satisfactory one both as a woman and as a medium. "It's amazing how people accept things once you've accepted them yourself," she says. "Two people left the foundation. Everyone else has been most supportive. Actually I think the age thing has been rather inspirational to other women. They see it working for us and that gives them courage to try an unconventional alternative. Why not? Happiness is so fleeting. Mere convention is hardly enough to warrant missing a chance at it. Of course I am startled sometimes in stores when someone refers to Greg as my son, but what difference does it make? This is the first man-woman relationship that I've ever experienced. It's also the first real closeness that I've ever shared on an adult level with a man.

"It's very exciting to watch Greg develop his own psychic gifts. Things seem to come to him so easily, while I've had to work very hard. That's one of the reasons why I'm sure our marriage was meant to be—just one more evolvement in the divine plan. Years ago I complained to Uvalla about what a hard time I was having. 'Why do I have to go through so much?' I asked.

" 'So that you will be able to help your husband who will become one of the greatest channels the world has ever known,' he replied. I couldn't understand that at all because Chris quit meditating after two years. He believed in the whole idea and was very supportive but couldn't seem to progress himself. Uvalla's answer just didn't make sense to me. He'd neglected to say *which* husband!

"Then shortly after Greg and I first met, the channel told him that he would be married within a year and have two children. We assumed that something had gotten scrambled. But there he was a year later married and helping to raise my two young ones. *Of course, it had to be right.*"

This sense of purpose and continuity continues to be the dominant force in Betty's life. She describes it as a kind of spiritual partnership. Trust is an essential factor. "They don't show me a blueprint. I haven't the faintest idea what's coming next," she admits. "The doors just open and I walk through. The channels could close down tomorrow forever, perhaps they will, but that's all right, too. Someone a lot smarter than I has the situation well in hand."

Irene Hickman

A Once in a Lifeline Experience

Is there death after life or a new beginning? Does existence end when the heart stops beating? Or will unfinished business remain until finally resolved?

Dr. Irene Hickman, a physician specializing in psychosomatic medicine, has devoted much of her life to helping troubled patients tote up what she is convinced are multilife accounts. The most frequently used tool is hypnosis.

"I don't believe in reincarnation. I *know* it to be a fact," she says with the calm confidence of one who has put her professional life on the line to stand up for her ideals.

During the 1960s Dr. Hickman ran for and was elected to the office of Sacramento (California) County assessor. Her platform was one of tax reform, controversial enough in itself. Friends and party members urged discretion, but the new assessor refused to be muzzled.

"I guess I'm a kind of female Patton," she admitted at the time, in reference to the volatile World War II general, also an exponent of reincarnation, whose views often provoked the ire of the Establishment. "I know that public officials aren't supposed to believe in reincarnation or at least not to admit it if they do, but my knowledge of past lives is much too implicit to suppress for political or professional purposes."

Because of her frankness, Irene Hickman's life has been a catalyst, generating personal and public assessment of social and political issues. Many conservative voters, emotionally threatened by the implications of reincarnation, became suspicious of her tax proposals as well. At one time a petition was circulated to impeach the assessor. There was a bomb threat against her home and a stone statue in her garden was disfigured by splashes of paint. After many accusations and attendant newspaper headlines, a recall election was held.

In 1966 Irene Hickman—then a political unknown—had surprised everyone by soundly defeating a popular and well-entrenched incumbent. Two years later in the recall election she received many more votes than in her initial triumph. It was a moral victory as well as a political one.

An attractive, opulent blonde who looks much younger than her sixty years, Irene Hickman has weathered the storms well but remains philosophical about her surprising success. Life to her is a learning process continued through numerous millennia. "Past lives are really *F* reports," she says. "We've failed somewhere or we wouldn't be here. Hopefully we acquire knowledge along the way."

She recalls a life in Palestine during the time of Christ. "I was a child then and watched while Jesus blessed the other children. I wanted to go forward for a blessing, too, but was too shy. Imagine being too shy for Jesus! That's really bad off. I've come a long way since then."

No one would have termed Irene Hickman shy when she faced the voting public and emphatically spoke out for

Irene Hickman

her beliefs. Faith in the concept of reincarnation has shaped and fortified her own life as well as enabling her to go one step beyond orthodox medical treatment in aiding her patients. "There was nothing else for me to do but come out flat-footedly and say it as I saw it," she explained later.

Having never been a closet reincarnationist, she would have found it impossible to become one in office. During the campaign, dedicated workers had eagerly related their dreams to the candidate while folding pamphlets and stuffing envelopes. Rather than plotting in traditional smoke-filled rooms, Irene Hickman's political cohorts enjoyed a kind of group therapy with psychic overtones. Once elected, the new assessor retained the same frank, innovative approach to problem solving that had marked her medical career.

Whether dissenting individuals believed in the concept of reincarnation seemed of little importance to her. Irene Hickman had personally derived sustenance from the philosophy and had seen the process of hypnotic regression free a multitude of patients from a variety of ailments. What else mattered? Irene had only to recall one of her most dramatic cures to receive instant reassurance that her beliefs and methods could be beneficial to many.

In 1959 while giving a public demonstration of hypnotism at the Fair Oaks Community Center in Sacramento, Dr. Hickman called for volunteers from the audience. Anne Armstrong, a housewife in her late thirties, raised her hand. Physician and subject had never met before.

Explaining that she had suffered severe migraine headaches since the age of seven, Mrs. Armstrong climbed onto the stage and then stood quietly before the doctor. She was desperate to overcome the misery that had defied medical aid and was greatly restricting her daily life. Frantic for any treatment that would provide even momentary respite, she had come to the demonstration at the suggestion of a neighbor who had heard of the many cures

Dr. Hickman had effected through hypnotherapy.

Anne Armstrong quickly forgot the audience around her. Within a few moments she had relaxed into a deep hypnotic trance. "Now let's go to the beginning of the headaches," Dr. Hickman suggested. "When and where did it all start?"

Suddenly, to the astonishment of everyone, the subject began to shriek in anguished terror. She had instantly bypassed adult life and even childhood experiences, plunging backward through an abyss of time to a previous existence in ancient Rome. The life revealed to the amazed audience was that of an entirely different entity. With sudden clarity the personality of Antonius emerged. The memories reached by hypnotic suggestion were of the final hours of the young man's life as he was being tortured on a rack.

Quickly reacting to the urgency of the moment, Dr. Hickman calmed the subject, suggesting that she should cry all she "needed to cry" and then awaken feeling rested and relaxed. A few moments later Anne Armstrong was herself again. Composed and refreshed, she eagerly made an appointment to see Dr. Hickman the following day at the Hickman Psychotherapy Center.

Through hypnosis, the full story of Antonius unfolded and was recorded as Anne Armstrong related it. It is a tragic narrative of a superb athlete who was the protégé and bodyguard of Julius Caesar. Those who conspired against Caesar viewed his strong, young protector as a formidable obstacle. The young man whose loyalty to the emperor was unquestioned had to be removed.

Antonius was subsequently framed, arrested, and then tortured. The tragedy culminated in his being dragged by the neck behind a chariot until he was dead. Instrumental in this brutal action was a foppish individual whom Antonius had disdainfully nicknamed "Fancy Pants." After working with the patient for a time, delving more deeply into the final trauma of Antonius and ultimately alleviating much—but not all—of the woman's present discomfort, Dr. Hickman said at last:

"I wonder what Antonius did to 'Fancy Pants' to deserve his end?"

The patient was at first reluctant to explore this possibility. "I don't think I want to know—at least not yet," she demurred.

But after a time Anne Armstrong decided that it was essential to know the whole truth, however unpleasant. Through additional hypnotic sessions she was able to transcend time even farther, slipping backward hundreds of years to a period when she had been responsible for the death of "Fancy Pants," then a slave—in a particularly gruesome fashion. The complete story of Anne Armstrong, her regression into the three lifetimes which have shaped her present life, and the psychic abilities she has developed as a result are related in another chapter.

Dr. Hickman was pleased but not at all surprised by her patient's new freedom from the migraine headaches that had plagued her for more than thirty years. The implications of the story of Antonius, with its affinity to karmic law, did not startle her in the least. The doctor had been committed to the possibility of regression as a therapeutic tool since 1958. Her initial interest in reincarnation was the result of reading *Many Mansions*, Gina Cerminara's carefully researched biography of Edgar Cayce.

Cayce, a very simple man of orthodox religion and little formal education, had cured himself of a severe throat ailment through self-hypnosis. Soon others were coming to him for treatment of their ailments. "I don't know anything about medicine," the baffled man insisted. Yet under hypnosis he was able to spell difficult medical terms of which he was totally unaware during the waking state. After literally thousands of successful diagnoses and subsequent cures, Cayce came to believe that he had somehow plugged in to a cosmic stream of information available to him only while in a hypnotic trance. The source of the information was totally apart from both his conscious and unconscious minds and had nothing to do with his own knowledge or personality—the entity that was Edgar Cayce.

As time passed, the "stream" also yielded information about the subjects' past lives which the entranced Cayce relayed to a stenographer. Reading over the words that his own mouth had uttered, he was aghast at revelations totally at variance with his own rigidly fundamentalist religious training.

At first, against his own inclinations, Cayce reluctantly yielded to the entreaties of his subjects, who found great insight in his readings of their past lives, readings which helped with career planning as well as alleviating stressful situations or relationships. Later, as his own past lives began to unfold, Cayce discovered many of the answers that had previously eluded him and developed a sense of purpose within his own life and a harmony with the universe.

After reading many of Cayce's case histories, Dr. Hickman and an associate became intrigued by the possibilities of reincarnation and medicine. "I'm not the kind of person that can automatically believe something just because I've read it in a book," she says in retrospect. "I was very intrigued by the possibilities but wanted to try them out myself. It seemed that if Edgar Cayce could do it, so could we. At first my friend and I were a little concerned that experiencing hypnosis might mean relinquishing our own free wills. Since neither of us were anxious to do this, we decided that we could prevent the possibility best by taking turns. Whatever relinquishment might have taken place could be retrieved when it was our own turn to act as hypnotist.

"The very first experience that came to me as a result of this early experiment with hypnosis was the revelation of a past life as the son of a southern planter during and after the Civil War. It was a shattering insight that struck a responsive chord in my present life. The man I had been, despite his family wealth and social position, had few friends. Parents and other relatives were remote, absorbed in their own lives. Servants waited on him merely for a paycheck. They might be perfunctory or obsequious but rarely caring. His only real friend was Joe, a black boy whose affection was deep and sincere, untouched by a sense of obligation or thoughts of his own benefit. Childhood recollections of playing with Joe were very vivid, but as the boy grew to manhood he escaped more and more frequently into a half world that contained little more than the four walls of his library. In his loneliness he had become a recluse. I saw myself as that man, unable to communicate with others, surrounding myself with books and papers until I'd withdrawn completely from the outside world.

"This memory seemed to explain my strong attachment for black people. They were rarely seen in the rural area of Iowa where I grew up. One might have expected that a small girl would be frightened or ill at ease in their presence; but, instead, whenever I saw a black person I had an urge to go up and throw my arms around whoever it might be. I also remembered a slight animosity or distrust of extremely wealthy people, though there had been nothing in my background to explain such a sensation. These reactions had always seemed a little strange to me even as I experienced them. Now I felt a new sense of continuity transcending what I'd always thought of as life. I also knew that it was not given to me to withdraw from others or from the realities of day-today living in this current existence."

The previous incarnation revealed that same fateful Sunday afternoon to Dr. Hickman's friend—a young bacteriologist—was also that of a male. She had been born before as the son of an Indian prince and, under hypnosis, described being given an elephant as a gift on her/his tenth birthday and at the same time being pledged to marry a woman to further her/his father's political ambitions.

"It's hard to discuss the his-her business when it comes to regression," Irene admits. "Each entity may alternate many times to learn various lessons." As a result of the information revealed through numerous regressions, she has come to view reincarnation as a learning process and insists that there is no escape from that process. "A man who gets a girl pregnant and then jilts her for another woman will surely be jilted in another lifetime, or he himself will be born an illegitimate child; or possibly he and the other woman will be born homosexual, unable to consummate their love with a child."

Irene Hickman theorizes that homosexuals are souls that have been born too quickly to adjust to a change of sex. "Imagine yourself as a woman waking suddenly to find herself in a man's body or a man trapped in a woman's form," she suggests.

"We change sex to satisfy some karmic requirement. Rarely are new characters introduced into the karmic scheme of things. We don't marry strangers or have affairs with them either. Seldom do we become involved with anyone that we haven't known before; yet each life is a new chance. What is done with that chance is up to the individual."

Determining that there was a definite healing potential in hypnotism and regression, Irene Hickman then slowly began to develop a technique of treatment. "Hypnosis is not difficult to do," she says. "Anyone with a little practice can learn the method. But it should not be attempted indiscriminately. Past life experiences may surface rapidly and can be hard for a novice to handle."

While most people would prefer to think of themselves as having lived glamorous lives, Irene rarely finds this to be the case in actual treatment. The fact that the stories revealed are so often ugly or squalid only adds to their validity, she believes. It's so natural for anyone to select lofty circumstances for himself. Yet the previous incarnations revealed under hypnosis are generally quite the opposite.

A classic example is that of Jane C., a forty-year-old typist whose drinking problem was so severe that by three each afternoon she was forced to leave her office to go to a nearby bar. Jane had somehow managed to keep the extent of her illness a secret from her husband and young daughter but could no longer ignore it herself. The dependence on liquor had developed as Jane sought to escape a blinding fear of the unknown. She felt herself to be damned, but could not fathom the reason. What had she done? What was the cause of the sudden panic that descended upon her for no apparent reason?

In an effort to overcome her unexplained terror and to curb her total reliance on alcohol, Jane had sought the services of a psychologist who shared clinic facilities with Irene Hickman. He, like his associate, was enthusiastic about hypnosis as a tool. Both agreed that hypnosis could bring into the conscious mind events and material which were unlikely to be recalled by other methods. He allowed that an individual could be regressed to early childhood, even to birth itself, but found the possibility of anything beyond totally unacceptable.

He had initially found Jane an excellent subject for hypnosis. In his three or four sessions with her, the psychologist had been able to lead her into a deep trance state but was surprised when nothing of significance surfaced. Now he suggested that Jane describe to him a time in her life when she had vividly experienced panic. To his surprise, she responded to this suggestion by replying that her name was Susan McDonald. Growing more specific, she spoke of a husband named Johnny who preferred to spend his money drinking at a tavern called Gleesbeck's while she and their small daughter, Annie, went hungry.

The psychologist hurriedly dismissed this statement as something Jane had read or seen in a movie. Patiently he attempted to return her thoughts to "reality," to the description of her present fears and sense of impending doom. His frustration increased as the patient continued to insist that she was Susan McDonald. Speaking with a slight Scots accent, Jane told a sordid tale of a family brawl that ended with her own death. Susan McDonald's nagging had so enraged her drunken husband that he had knocked her to the floor. She was killed accidentally when her head struck the leg of a stove.

Dr. Hickman, entering the room unexpectedly, heard the patient's voice raised in impatience and bewilderment. "I told you," Jane cried, "it's the seventeenth of April in 1780. I'm dead! I'm right here on the floor!"

The psychologist was equally impatient and bewildered. Jane C. simply would not return to being Jane C. Fortunately his colleague felt no such compunction to remain with the known, the readily explainable. Dr. Hickman quickly switched on a tape recorder and leaned forward. "This is Irene," she introduced herself in a quiet, even tone. "I understand. You died in 1780."

The tense, angry expression on Jane's face changed to one of curious expectation. The 1780 scene has been replaced in her mind.

In the taped interview that followed, Jane first recalled her original birth experience in this lifetime—an existence that followed the one previously highlighted. Jane had apparently endured a long waiting period before being allowed to incarnate again. "They're pulling me out of my mother," she explained in frightened tones and then more calmly, as though watching a scene enacted before her, described a bearded man wearing glasses, who was her mother's physician.

As a newborn infant, Jane was aware of preferences that seemed to follow from one life to another. When her grandmother brought her a bottle, she registered dismay, thinking: "I never did like warm cow's milk and now here it is and there's nothing that I can do about it." But much more serious was the sense of having returned to earth to rid herself of a desperate fear centered within herself.

Dr. Hickman quickly focused on the fear. "Can you feel it in your stomach?" she asked.

"No, it's not in my stomach. It's right here," Jane corrected her, placing her hand on the center of her chest. (Dr. Hickman cites this as a valid refutation of the claim that a subject merely responds to the suggestions of the therapist. Jane's responses were often a direct contradiction of her own previous suggestions.)

Jane went on to describe a childhood that seemed an ironic replay of her previous tragic existence. "Here we go again," she remarked as though watching a movie. Now it was Jane's father who drank and her mother who nagged. With no suggestion from the therapist the hypnotized patient had quickly made the connection, relating the events of her present lifetime with what appeared to be her past. Once again there had been violence. This time the angry quarrels climaxed with her father's suicide before Jane's very eyes when she was six years old. The family bitterness that followed left her even more confused and frightened than she had been at birth.

Skillfully Irene calmed the patient. "You are feeling fear and hate about something that happened a long time ago. But it isn't necessary to feel that hate now. You will come back to the present time and place, and you will awake feeling relaxed and comfortable. You may remember some of the things we have been talking about, but nothing will disturb or alarm you. You will feel relief from the fear, the hate, the sadness. They will all be gone as you return to the present time. You will awake as I count from ten to one. At one you will be awake and you will feel fine. Ten, nine, eight, seven, six, five, four, three, two, one. Awake!"

Jane opened her eyes slowly and smiled. "I feel so much better. Thank you," she said, leaning back comfortably. The tense lines about her face had disappeared.

"Is the fear gone?" Dr. Hickman asked.

"A lot of it, but there is still some left," Jane admitted.

"Don't worry, we'll work on that some more tomorrow," Dr. Hickman reassured her.

The following day found Jane eagerly awaiting her appointment. Both the psychologist and Dr. Hickman had arranged their schedules so that they could be present. Dr. Hickman would now preside as the hypnotherapist, with him sitting in. He was intrigued but still skeptical.

Jane dropped quickly into the trance state and, without warning, still another incarnation manifested itself. This was Sahri, an unfortunate girl who had been orphaned by Armenian terrorists and then sold into slavery during the fourteenth century. Sahri's master, Abn, was a repulsively fat man who mistreated the girl so cruelly that she ultimately killed herself at eighteen to escape his sexual perversions.

"Is this when the fear began?" Dr. Hickman asked her entranced subject.

"No," was the prompt, emphatic reply.

"Then go back to the time when the fear first started," the doctor urged. "I will count slowly from one to seven. While I'm counting, you will go back farther and farther to the time when the fear first began. Once we've found the origin, we can take it all away. One, two, three, four, five, six, seven. Look around you and tell me, your friend and helper, what is happening. I can hear you but I can't see what you see. So tell me what is happening."

In this manner Dr. Hickman regressed Jane beyond Sahri's tragic life to yet another existence, to the life of Maureen O'Flaherty, which appears to be the original personality.

"Tell me what you see," she encouraged.

"A little hut with a thatched roof, a chicken, and a white goat," Jane answered. "My name is Maureen."

Slowly emerged the personality of Maureen, a spirited Irish girl residing near Belfast in the twelfth century. A brutal experience which she had endured in her fifteenth year was the cause of problems in Maureen's lifetime and in subsequent existences. Naive and inexperienced, Maureen had fallen in love with a young neighbor, Tim Dugan, and yielded to his sexual advances. The quiet harmony of her life was destroyed forever by Maureen's outraged parents. Tim shattered her innocent pleasure in the discovery of love when he abandoned her to their angry retribution. Within a few hours Maureen's entire world had been turned upside down, leaving her confused and desolate.

Maureen was starved and severely beaten. "You'll never do that again!" her father threatened as the heavy leather strap rose and fell. The entity's fears began at this time and with them a sense of bitter resentment. Tim was gone and her father had beaten her until the blood ran, but there would be other men! She became promiscuous, creating a vicious chain reaction for herself. Maureen's short, sad life ended at thirty-seven with another violent death.

"He had red hair and a red beard," Jane calmly described the murderer of her spiritual ancestor. "I laughed at him and he choked me. He didn't understand that I was really laughing at my father. But it didn't make any difference. I was ready. It was no kind of life anyway."

As Jane related her experiences while under hypnosis, ventilating her repressed fears by repetitive discussion, a happy relaxed woman replaced the half-hysterical creature who had first presented herself for treatment. Jane was literally a different person.

"My associate was *almost* a different person," Irene recalls. "He wanted to believe but remained a skeptic. 'It could still be a fantasy or scenes created to please herself or her therapist,' he insisted."

Then, as today, she feels such possibilities are highly unlikely. "There was nothing complimentary to Jane in the material, nothing protective, nothing which would indicate that the subject was attempting to conceal something," she maintains. "For me to assume that the material disclosed in the sessions was a fantasy seems more illogical than to believe that it came from a pre-existence period. But that's not the point anyway. One doesn't have to believe in reincarnation to use regression material to help the patient, and if it works—what else matters?

"Certainly Jane had enough violence in this present lifetime to fill her entire being with fear. For the first six years of her life she had witnessed a constant clash of wills between her parents— two people who had callously admitted that they had never wanted her. On the day of her father's death she had been present at one last horrendous scene, had stood helplessly at the window watching her mother kicked and beaten until the snow was dark with her blood. She, her younger brother, and mother had fled only to be followed by her father who threatened suicide if they did not return home with him. Before Jane's very eyes, the man consumed poison and then fell to the floor writhing in agony until he was dead.

"It might be argued that this experience alone was the basis of Jane's fear and I'm sure many would take this position," Dr. Hickman admits. "Yet if this is so, why did Jane bother to create new fantasies even more dreadful than her remembered experiences?

"According to the material which Jane C. presented while entranced, it would seem that she had been involved in lives of violence with the same cast of characters for more than 800 years. During this time she had lived four lives—as Jane C., as Susan McDonald, as Sahri, and as Maureen O'Flaherty. Under hypnosis she had realized that the soul who had been her daughter, Annie, in 1780 had become her mother in 1922 and then had returned to life once more as her daughter, Gloria, in 1956. The entity who had been Tim, a boy who had loved and then deserted Maureen, became Susan's husband, Johnny, in the next life. Johnny, a violent man who allowed his family to suffer from cold and hunger and then finally killed his wife in a drunken rage, returned again to earth and became the unlucky Jane's father— another man given to drunken violence. The soul who had been Abn, the fat, ugly merchant who had bought Sahri in a slave market and then mistreated her so cruelly that she committed suicide, returned to life as Jane's younger brother, Robert, an entity the subject had hated instinctively since earliest childhood."

Dr. Hickman points out that each of Jane's lives was marked by murder or suicide, hate, lust, and squalor. It would seem that if the patient were going to fabricate a life for herself, she would have added something of love and beauty—qualities totally lacking in each of Jane's sordid existences.

But whether the material came from fantasy or reality, it served its purpose. Once Jane understood the basis of her fear and experienced a catharsis of the emotion attached to the memory, it vanished. Her drinking ceased, for it was no longer necessary to obscure a panic that did not exist. Realizing the cause of her lifetime animosity toward her brother, she determined to make peace—hoping to settle the score amicably for all eternity.

Jane recalled that as Susan she had sometimes become exasperated with Annie when the child cried for food and that she, desperately hungry herself, had often struck the girl. Knowing that the same entity had been her own unhappy mother, a woman who had frequently lashed out in anger and desperation, Jane resolved that the pitiful chain of frustration and misery would end with herself. Her own daughter, Gloria, would not suffer as Annie had done, only to act out the same miserable script in another lifetime.

It would seem that—real or imagined—the past life experiences of Susan, Sahri, and Maureen have had a very positive effect upon Jane C. and her family in *this* lifetime.

Solomon Grundy. Born on Monday. Christened on

Tuesday. Married on Wednesday. Took ill on Thursday.
Worse on Friday. Died on Saturday. Buried on Sunday.
And that was the end of Solomon Grundy.

So goes the rhyme that all of us have heard and many
accept as a frivolous yet factual summation of reality. From
earliest childhood Irene Hickman has dismissed this prosaic possibility as improbable. She was and is confident that
there is a purpose implicit in the human existence.

Born the eighth of nine children, she showed an early
predisposition to learning and could read and write before
entering kindergarten. But far more striking was a gift of
sensing truth. She describes this recognition as a physical
sensation, referring to it often as her "buzz." Almost from
babyhood Irene recalls that when an anecdote was told or a
story read that was true, her buzz would alert her with a
kind of tingle starting at the top of her head and spreading
slowly over her body. The buzz produced a visible reaction
as well as a sensual one, causing chill bumps.

This sense of knowing may have sustained the girl
through a very difficult childhood. Her mother died before
Irene was eleven years old. Her father, unimpressed by his
daughter's intellectual gifts, felt that education was wasted
on a girl. Despite his pressure on her to remain at home,
Irene was the only one in the family to graduate from high
school. Eager for more knowledge, she left home at sixteen
and proceeded to work her way through college by reading
palms in a Des Moines tearoom. The strange, unexplained
facility for foretelling the future had developed after reading a book on palmistry at age twelve and had grown with
the years.

A marriage during her junior year to a young divinity
student did not stop Irene from completing college.
Twelve stormy years of marriage followed, during which
time she had two sons and then entered medical school—
once more working to pay all her own expenses, though
this time at more pedestrian occupations. She was divorced

during her senior year, retaining custody of the two boys, who were then seven and ten years old. A year later, in 1951, she was married to Jack Hickman and later had another son while continuing to practice medicine.

During the preceding long unhappy years, Irene had become increasingly aware of how thoughts and feelings affect general health. The certainty that tensions created by an unfortunate childhood and first marriage had produced physical disturbances within her own body had stimulated an interest in psychosomatic medicine.

"So many times when prescribing drugs for a patient I would experience a sense of frustration," she recalls today. "I felt that I was not really doing what was needed, that I should be going at the problem from a psychological approach rather than merely treating symptoms."

A growing interest in the possibilities inherent in hypnosis eventually changed the direction of her practice to the sometimes controversial field of psychosomatic medicine while furnishing her with the tool to get at the hidden causes of many physical problems.

One of numerous success stories was that of Margaret Tellez, a bookkeeper employed by Aerojet Corporation in Sacramento, who came to Dr. Hickman in 1959. Margaret was all but incapacitated by an allergy to cold water. She couldn't wash vegetables or lingerie or even hold a frosty glass without breaking out in large hives. The inside of her throat would swell if she drank a cold liquid, and raindrops would cause not only her face, hands, and legs to erupt into hives but her whole body as well. Clothing was no protection once the allergy had been activated.

Margaret was referred by her family doctor to a dermatologist, who found her condition so severe and so completely baffling that he in turn referred her to his former medical school professor. Unable to cure the allergy, the second dermatologist invited Margaret to be the guest of the Stanford Lane Hospital in San Francisco while she was studied under ideal laboratory conditions. Margaret remained in the hospital one week, during which time she was presented to the entire staff at grand rounds. Her hands were wired with electrodes, she was placed inside a plastic vacuum for observation, and numerous blood samples were taken.

Though totally fascinated by the case, the many doctors who had come to study Margaret were unable to find a cure. They were in agreement on one thing only: Margaret's condition was very serious. She was warned never to shower unless someone else was in the house, for it was feared that a sudden accidental change to a cold temperature could prove fatal. A series of shots were finally prescribed and Margaret was discharged. If anything, the allergy was worse.

At the suggestion of a friend, the troubled woman decided to consult Irene Hickman. She made the appointment reluctantly and only because it appeared to be her last resort. Margaret had heard of Dr. Hickman's past-life regressions and was upset by their implications, which were in direct conflict with the highly orthodox religious teachings of her childhood. Decent people didn't come back in new bodies. They waited obediently in their graves until awakened by the Lord.

Despite her fears, Margaret slipped quickly into a hypnotic trance. As if from a great distance, she could hear her own voice relating a terrifying chronicle of tragic experiences involving water. These transcended her current life existence by hundreds of years.

Recalling this dramatic breakthrough today, Margaret Tellez says, "First I saw myself as a little girl playing in an apple orchard while my older brother gathered fruit. He didn't realize how close I was to the bank of a deep river. I lost my footing and fell in, drowning before he even realized that I was missing.

"Once I was trapped inside a sinking ship and drowned, while in another lifetime I was able to escape from a sinking ship with two of my children but watched helplessly as the ship went down, taking my other two babies with it.

"In still a different life it was I who was responsible for someone else's death by drowning. This time I was a galley slave on a ship and participated with other slaves in a revolt in which we overpowered the drummer whose insistent beat had forced us to row ever faster. We beat him unmercifully and then forced him over the side, keelhauling him until dead."

Margaret Tellez went six times to Dr. Hickman in order to work out her problems. Under hypnosis she talked freely of her four traumatic experiences. The idea of reincarnation was no longer alarming, for she had come to accept the experiences as fact, a part of the sum total of herself like a ready smile or a preference for cream.

"That was then; this is now," she was finally able to say. *"I don't have to have these allergies and I'm not going to have them."* She reports today—nearly twenty years later—that the condition disappeared immediately after her decision and has never returned.

An exciting spin-off of Margaret's cure was an increased psychic awareness that developed after her successful treatment. "Psychic ability is natural to us all," Dr. Hickman believes, "but big lumps of emotion have blocked it. These have to come out before each individual can use his or her own gifts. That's where I come in. I'm like a pick-and-shovel detail."

In an effort to grow personally and to find new methods of helping her troubled patients, Irene has experimented with a number of approaches to inner reality. In comparing the numerous therapy modes available, she says: "If you think of the patient as a beautifully carved Japanese chest whose original design is almost completely obscured by layers and layers of varnish, then you get some idea of what the therapist is up against.

"Psychoanalysis is like chipping away at the varnish a flake at a time. If the patient can afford it and the doctor lives long enough, it may ultimately be possible to get down to the essential truths. Hypnosis works much faster. It's like paint remover and can wash off a whole layer of covering at a time. Inhalation therapy is even more penetrating. It serves as a kind of blowtorch, removing several layers at once. But the most dramatic effects are achieved with LSD, which takes even less time. LSD is like an atom reactor that blows off all coverings at once, leaving the individual bare naked in all his glory and garbage."

In preparation for experimenting personally with LSD therapy at the International Foundation for Advanced Study in Menlo Park, California, Dr. Hickman underwent a series of eight weekly interviews. During this preliminary screening, she received psychiatric and psychological testing to determine her adaptability to the drug. A part of the determination process was the inhalation of carbogen, a mixture of 70 per cent oxygen and 30 per cent carbon dioxide. This was designed by the foundation to accustom the subject to the regressive loss of ego boundaries that he or she would experience more fully during the LSD experiment.

While experimenting with carbogen, Irene perceived the insight that she had selected her own parents before birth, knowing that as their child she would be forced to develop the self-reliance which would be essential in later life. "I could still have developed the necessary self-reliance, but would have had a happier childhood if I hadn't been so impatient," she considered. "I shouldn't have been in such a rush to come back."

Dr. Hickman later used carbogen on her own patients when hypnosis proved ineffective. A testimonial to the effectiveness of this method was James J., a twenty-seven-year-old stock clerk employed by the State of California. The man could function well enough when working quietly in the supply room of a government building. He could converse easily with men or even with older women so long as the subject matter remained impersonal and unemotional; but when he attempted to relate to a woman of his own age on any conversational level, he was totally incapacitated by his own stuttering. As a result, James's life had been lonely and without color. Since growing to manhood he had slipped into an isolated existence, while longing inwardly for friendship with women and sexual contact.

When James J. did not respond to hypnosis, Irene decided to use carbogen. The mask was applied to the patient's face and he inhaled deeply. Responding quickly, he was suddenly carried back in time to a previous existence in early California. In this incarnation James was an entirely different type of man, a dashing Don Juan who had no difficulties whatsoever with women. In fact, the entity was so glib that his many easy conquests had grown boring.

"It was not a matter of a girl in every port," Dr. Hickman relates. "It was several girls in every port. So adept was he at enticing and seducing these hapless creatures that he turned to married women. Not only did they possess the added lure of forbidden fruit but also had husbands for him to outwit. This ultimate challenge finally proved his undoing. The selfish, manipulative entity who later became the timid, stammering James J. was finally discovered in bed with a married woman and was subsequently hanged."

When James J. was confronted by his own voice on tape relating this rather squalid tale, he could readily comprehend the irony of his present situation. The stuttering that had prevented him from enjoying even the most casual relationship with a young woman had been a means of paying off a karmic debt. With comprehension came release. "That was a different man, a different life, a different century," he reasoned. "I don't have to suffer any longer and I don't have to make the same mistakes."

James' tension disappeared. He was able to talk easily with women and immediately began to date. But knowing what he did about the past, James' attitude was one of appreciation and responsibility rather than exploitation. He knew the unhappy penalty for his previous indiscretions and was determined not to make the same mistake again.

Irene took the dramatic step beyond hypnosis and inhalation therapy on October 14, 1963, when she was administered LSD at the International Foundation for Advanced Study. Dr. Mary Hughes Allen, a psychiatrist now in private practice, was part of the two-person team who remained with Irene throughout the session.

As with other subjects who availed themselves of the foundation's research program, she spent the day listening to music and viewing various visual stimuli such as family photographs, pictures of different kinds of scenery and flowers. She remained under twenty-four hour supervision and was seen in follow-up interviews at one day, one week, two, four, eight, twelve, and twenty-four weeks after the LSD experience.

The stated expectation of both the foundation and Irene was that she would have an experience in which she could learn something about herself that would prove useful to her and would permit her to alter life in a more self-fulfilling direction. The concept underlying this approach is that an individual can have a single insight so profound and impressive that her life experience in the months and years that follow will become a continuing growth process.

That a single overwhelming experience can have such far-reaching results is not commonly accepted by psychotherapists, although studies of religious conversions have suggested the possibility. Irene's experiences would tend to indicate that it could. She certainly feels that it has.

"I went into the LSD experience with the intention of playing it for everything it was worth," she wrote nine days after taking a combination of LSD and mescaline. "I asked for it and it happened. If there is more, I cannot at the moment conceive of the possibility. To picture graphically all of the visual experiences would require at least ten thousand years of painting one picture a day. The paints used would have to be of the substance of rainbows and brilliant gems, the silt of the stars, golden sunlight, and the power of God.

"The most surprising aspect of it was the immensity. It was so much larger than I expected. There was a little apprehension and reluctance to go all the way at first, but this soon left. I realized that I could have stopped the experience at a number of levels, but chose each time to go on."

Plunging backward in time, she was able to check the past life experiences that had previously been revealed to her through hypnosis. She saw herself as the southern planter's son, as the child in Palestine staring wistfully at Jesus, as a sister of Nefertiti in Egypt, and then again in Egypt—this time as a Jewish slave during the era of Moses. With her in the latter incarnation—as she and they themselves had always believed—were her husband, Jack, and their son, Alan. "Alan and I were slaves who helped Moses in the Exodus. Jack was an Egyptian overseer more interested in the pretty Jewish women than in maintaining discipline," she recalls.

"No wonder Egypt is so very fascinating," she said aloud to Dr. Allen during the LSD session. But then Irene went on beyond the isolated instances of her own birth and rebirth to universal creation. As an aftermath of the ingestion of the drug, she felt the agony of the earth being torn by war and experienced the delicate iridescence of a soap bubble. She examined destructiveness, hate, and greed and found them a shadow part of the whole cosmic harmony. She visited the primal sea of the universe and watched God's first wave bring it into being, and then she listened raptly as the organ of the universe blasted forth its perfection of color and harmony.

Writing of this illumination nearly twelve years later, Irene says: "My forty-eight years—at that time—on this earth were like a tiny grain of dust as compared with the

LSD experience, which was greater than the entire cosmos. After the experiment I became aware that I knew what others were thinking or feeling, but tried to ignore this gift as best I could. I felt that it would be disturbing to others if they knew their inner thoughts could be so monitored; besides, the monitoring itself was largely unpleasant for me. So much pain was included in the material that I received. There was beauty, too; but even that troubled me as I felt like a trespasser. The most uncomfortable aspect of this phase was knowing what was going on within my own family. I was relieved when this ability slowly began to fade and I could turn it off more and more frequently until it disappeared entirely.

"In recent years there has been a gradual return of this kind of sensitivity until now it has reached a comfortable level—helpful for obtaining inner guidance but without the detailed invasion of privacy that I found so unpleasant. I am convinced that what I experienced that day was all that ever was or is or ever can be from the beginning of time. It was nice to have the opportunity to check on my past lives and I did this briefly. Finding that they merged with previous information, I went on to far more important things. I discovered that I could run history back and forth and watch it all unfold before my eyes whether I had personally lived at that time or not.

"I could and did check on philosophical and religious concepts and discovered the Edgar Cayce findings to be correct. Cayce's statement that the initiates had known the truth from the beginning had always puzzled me. Now I understood. I recognized a portion of the LSD-induced sensations as being from earlier initiation experiences in other bodies, but this new experience took me much farther than I had ever been before. There is no doubt that still greater initiations are possible, but for me this is sufficient. I don't think that anyone who had the illumination that I have had would need or want to repeat it," she concluded.

One might feel rather dubious about a therapeutic

procedure which leads to a sort of otherworldliness or to dropping out from life. But members of the foundation dispelled this idea entirely in an article which appeared in the November-December 1962 issue of the *Journal of Neuropsychiatry*. Sharing a joint byline were J. N. Sherwood, M.D.; W. W. Harmon, Ph.D., and M. J. Stolaroff, associate director of research at the foundation. "Such a tendency has not been observed in our subjects," they wrote. "On the contrary, their experiences have usually led to the discovery of added meaning and zest in their lives in this world."

Irene Hickman was no exception. As an aftermath of her LSD experience, she felt impelled to enter politics. "At first I was reluctant to do it," she admits. "My practice and family had always kept me very busy; yet I felt quite strongly that this was part of my karmic destiny and that taking LSD had given me the necessary courage and confidence in myself—not to mention the insight—to know that it was essential that I go ahead.

"Prior to the experiment I had brought a lawsuit against the current assessor, Richard Blechschmidt, in an effort to force him to assess everybody equally. I had hoped to obtain a court order forcing equality in county assessment, but the judge ruled against me. This came after the LSD experience. In handing down the verdict, he said, 'If the homeowners don't like the way they are being taxed, they can elect a new assessor.' Now it seemed that those words were aimed straight at me. I knew that I'd signed up for this 'course' before birth. Now, whether I was ready or not, the doors were opening and I had to go through."

Defeating Blechschmidt in 1966 on a platform of equalization and reform, Irene as Sacramento County assessor immediately began to put into practice the reforms that she had promised in her initial campaign. Her aim was to abolish all taxes on buildings and personal property. In their place would be a single tax on land in proportion to its value.

The land tax theoretically would force the best possible use of the land and eliminate the type of unproductive
speculator who lets land stand idle to increase in value—
especially if a nearby government project such as a high-
way is causing the rise. It would, she believed, eventually
do away with slums, for landlords would have a new
incentive to improve their property. People should be
rewarded for their production, Irene insisted, not taxed for
it.

Despite her own rather unsettling candor on behalf of
the medical use of LSD and the principles of reincarnation,
and the overt efforts of landed interests to unseat her,
Irene remained a popular administrator. At a time when
feminism was not in vogue, she was one of the first women
in California to hold a countywide office—despite the fact
that two men spent $32,000 to mount a massive recall
offensive against her.

Knowing there were many who feared the changes she
proposed because they didn't fully understand them, Irene
aired her views on a series of radio programs. Each ended
with the plea: "My door is always open. I am available by
phone, I am available to make talks to your club, your PTA,
or in your living room. I will accept all invitations. You will
be able to speak to me, to ask your questions, to challenge
what I have to say. I also challenge anyone who opposes my
ideas to debate me on radio, television, or public meeting.
I welcome opposition. I welcome challenge. I welcome
debate. The opposition has failed to accept my challenge.
Perhaps they have nothing to say."

Irene obviously had plenty to say. She said it to such
varying groups as the N.A.A.C.P., the Young Republicans,
the Knights of Columbus, the National Spacecraft Association, and the assembled faculty and students of Sacramento
State College. She did not succeed in everything that she
attempted to do in office, but several years later the ideas
that she ventilated so colorfully were beginning to take
effect. "Politics will never be the same in this town since

Irene," a reporter on the *Sacramento Union* said five years after her departure from office. "She was the most exciting thing that ever happened in the Sacramento Valley."

Today Irene Hickman has resumed medical practice and is living as quietly as it is possible for her to live in Williston, North Dakota. In addition to her medical duties, she leads a group that gathers in her home to discuss and analyze their dreams. "Dream analysis is an excellent place to begin," she says. "It's safer than hypnosis and can be handled by each person individually if necessary."

In reviewing the activities of her own life, she relates them to a three-ring circus. "I am the owner-operator of the circus," she says. "In one ring I function as a physician concerned with health—physical health, emotional health, mental health, and particularly how these relate to one another in what is called psychosomatic medicine.

"In the second ring of the circus are social-economic matters having to do with the health of our society as a whole. The third ring deals with understanding of a spiritual nature, the relationship to the universal mind, to God, the deity, whatever one chooses to call it. Sometimes two of the rings have merged, as when the principles of reincarnation or karma have entered into the solving of a medical problem. "I am not a researcher in the true sense of the word," she admits. "I don't have the time or resources to fly all over the world to investigate Margaret Tellez's drownings or to establish whether Anne Armstrong was really Antonius, or Jane C. lived a life as an Armenian slave girl or James J. was the nineteenth-century equivalent of Erol Flynn. Whether they were or weren't is really immaterial. My concern as a physician lies in curing the allergies, the headaches, the alcoholism, the stuttering, or whatever else the problem may be.

"For the patient, it is sufficient to be well again. For myself, I am content with my own philosophy. It has brought me great comfort. I feel a complete harmony with life knowing that I am the sum total of my past choices—

thoughts and desires, as well as acts. Understanding the karma that arises from these factors provides workable solutions to daily external problems. As assessor, for instance, it was much easier to deal more philosophically with various troublesome individuals after recognizing them from previous lives. The unfinished business aspect of it all made me stronger and more understanding.

"Within my own family it has helped as well. I have always been certain that my second son, Sherwood, was once my mother. Whenever I have found him lacking in thoughtfulness or consideration, I have always been reminded by the wee small voice within that I undoubtedly deserved every minute of it. This knowledge made it so much easier to change what I could in him as a wayward boy, but also to accept what could not be changed.

"If there is one thing I know, it is that I will return to earth again and again until I become a fitting companion for my creator and for others who have finally passed the course. I might as well just get on with the job of becoming perfect because that is my ultimate destiny—and the destiny of everyone else on this earth."

Anne Armstrong

An Explorer on the Sea of Time

Tiny, small-boned Anne Armstrong was startled to find herself suddenly locked within the brawny body of an athlete.

Little did she dream then that this shattering instant of awareness was the beginning of an odyssey through time and space that would one day project on the screen of her consciousness a whole mosaic of entities, each with its own personality to manifest, its own part to play, its own contribution to make. Nor could she realize that the sum total of all this experience would be a renaissance of psychic awareness within herself. She had embarked upon a mystical voyage that would encompass all eternity. The journey had only just begun, but already the voyager had begun to change. She could never be the same again.

But Anne was too overwhelmed by the moment to have any inkling of the enormous scope of the adventure

Anne Armstrong   C.J. Marrow

before her. "I'm not a girl any more!" she had announced in amazement. "I'm so big," she marveled, feeling her small arms and shoulders but sensing something much more massive. "I feel me, but I don't feel me. I'm tall and my arms and feet seem huge. I feel so strong!"

Irene Hickman watched her patient intently. "Who are you?" she asked. "Tell me about yourself. I can hear you but I can't see what you see. Can you tell me who you are?"

"I'm a young man," Anne replied, a note of probing concentration replacing the original surprise in her voice. "I'm twenty three. I have a handsome face and dark, curly hair. My eyes are blue." The petite Sacramento housewife paused a moment and then continued, "My name is Antonius and I'm a Roman."

Anne had asked to be hypnotized in the hope that her physician would be able to find a cause and a cure for the severe migraine headaches that had plagued her for more than thirty years. Hypnosis seemed the last resort after an endless series of visits to a variety of medical specialists who had prescribed an extensive and expensive number of treatments which had proved totally ineffectual.

After volunteering to be hypnotized at a public demonstration, Anne had become hysterical when told to regress to the time the headaches had first begun. When the physician, Irene Hickman, suggested that she come in for treatment, Anne had agreed with some reluctance. Fear of the unknown was balanced against her natural curiosity. A desire to be free of the fearsome headaches had been the deciding factor.

Now she relaxed on a couch in Dr. Hickman's office. Her eyes were closed as she described a scene presumably from another existence. "I'm all dressed up," she said. "I'm wearing a white toga trimmed with gold and a flowing cape. I'm standing beside an older man with a gold wreath around his head. I'm very close to this man, very devoted to him. We're standing on a kind of parapet as we watch a parade of soldiers going by beneath us. We seem to be reviewing troops. The man beside me is very important, very powerful."

"Now what's happening?" the doctor asked softly. Anne had paused in her narrative as though lost in the pageantry of the past.

"I'm talking to the man with the wreath, pleading with him, warning him—I think. He doesn't seem to listen. I'm growing frustrated, angry. Finally I turn my back and hurry down a flight of stairs. My horse is waiting outside and I ride away."

Suddenly Anne screamed in anguish as the scene appeared to shift. "I'm on a wheel and they're pulling it tighter and tighter," she moaned. "I can't stand it!" Her head moved frantically from side to side as though trying to escape pain.

Anne began to scream, long angonized shrieks that seemed to rise from the depth of her being. Dr. Hickman leaned forward and gently took her patient's hand. "This happened a long, long time ago. It's all over now. I will count to five and then you will awaken feeling refreshed. The pain will all be gone."

Anne emerged from the trance on command. Listening to the tape of her own voice, she shook her head in bewilderment. "That couldn't be me," she reasoned. "None of it makes any sense. I don't understand at all. I don't know anything about ancient Rome. I've never even been to modern Rome. And why should I see myself as a man?"

The doctor shook her head. Why indeed? Agreeing to meet Dr. Hickman again to continue the hypnotherapy, Anne discussed the experience that evening with her husband, Jim, an aerospace engineer. "It's very frightening," she admitted. "I'm afraid of what I may find out. There are so many questions unanswered. Do I really want to know the truth? Perhaps it's something ugly. Am I strong enough to face it?"

Jim could see no other course but to continue. "Do

you have any choice?" he asked. "No doctor has been able to cure your headaches. I've seen them grow worse with each passing year. Now here at last is hope for a cure. How can you even consider giving up?"

Anne sighed wearily. The migraines had been a draining experience which seemed to be relentlessly pulling her from the mainstream of life. Sometimes the agony was unendurable; yet this sudden challenge to her entire set of beliefs was equally threatening. Although she no longer attended church, Anne had been raised as a Catholic, instilled in childhood with religious precepts that die hard. Life on earth happened only once, she had been told. There was one chance and one chance only for eternal salvation. Christ had lived and died to make this clear to all who followed him on this earth. Now suddenly the whole tidy concept was challenged by an hour in a doctor's office. It was easy enough for Jim to shop around for new philosophies. Having no institutionalized religion, the idea of reincarnation posed no threat to him. It was merely a new possibility to consider, one selection from a philosophical smorgasbord. He possessed a scientist's passion for investigation and a fascination for the unknown—qualities that Anne admired; but, she reminded herself, he was not the one undergoing this psychic transformation. It was she who must face the ordeal alone. Past-life regression was a very existential experience, she was discovering. Anne had never felt more lonely.

Ultimately Jim's enthusiatic encouragement gave her the added courage necessary to continue her mystical search. At first the goal was merely a headache cure, but soon the stakes had broadened to encompass her identity in the cosmic scheme of things.

A week later the couple was sitting at home when Jim glanced idly at a book Anne had borrowed from a neighbor. Its topic was self-hypnosis. "If that doctor can hypnotize you, why can't I?" he mused aloud.

Anne was dubious.

"It says here that anyone can learn it," he insisted, waving the book at her. Jim compared several methods outlined in the table of contents, chose the one that sounded easiest, and switched on the tape recorder.

Within minutes he was recording. "This is October 14, 1959," he said. "Anne has gone to bed and is relaxed. I have counted to twenty-one and told her to go to sleep. She appears to be in a deep trance." Starting with her present age, he regressed her backward to birth, one year at a time. Then he suggested that she go back even further to a time before birth.

Suddenly Anne was talking excitedly of horses, dust, and chariots. Then her tone changed to one of intense pain. "They're dragging me!" she screamed. "Oh my head, my head, my head!" Her body relaxed as abruptly as it had stiffened. It seemed that Antonius had lost consciousness. "They've stopped the chariot," Anne explained. "They think that I'm dead, but I'm not. Oh, noooooooo! They're starting it again."

Frightened by her anguish, Jim hurriedly suggested that she awaken "feeling fine." This she was fortunately able to do. Afterward the two sat silently listening to a playback of Anne's pain-filled voice describing the tragic scene. Did my headache really begin 2000 years ago? Anne wondered, shivering at the thought of her broken body dragged by a chariot across the rough cobblestones.

She continued the search at the Hickman Psychotherapy Center a few days later. Once again the scene was the torture chamber of a Roman dungeon. Anne, deep into a hypnotic trance, began to moan pitifully.

"What are they doing to you?" Irene urged.

"Oh, I'm afraid to look. All I can do is feel."

"Why are they doing this to you?" the doctor persisted, but Anne merely shook her head. "Let's go forward in time and try to find out. It's an hour later now. Tell me what you see."

"A chariot. They're pulling me by the neck." Anne's

mouth was open, gasping for breath. Her hand was at her throat as though trying to relieve the pressure of a rope. "Oh, I want to die," she sobbed," but I shouldn't cry."

"Why shouldn't you cry?"

"Men don't cry," she said with lonely finality.

Anne began to cough and sputter. "It's so dusty," she complained. "I'm choking." The agonized coughing continued; then there was silence. "I'm free," Anne said at last in a calm, quiet voice. "I feel like I'm going out the top of my head. I'm dead now. But that poor body! It's so broken, so bloody. Someone just kicked it. They've untied it from the chariot and are walking away."

"Are you all right?"

"I'm fine. I'm just standing there looking down at the person I used to be. I feel clean and peaceful."

Anne awakened and for a time Antonius was allowed to recede into the past. In the days that followed, the headaches were much relieved but did not entirely disappear. The why of it all continued to intrigue Jim. He was determined to find answers to the psychic puzzle. Who was Antonius? Why had he been so cruelly treated and who was his tormentor? Anne, too, was excited by the experiment. She was no longer frightened by the implications of Antonius' existence and was now as eager as Jim and Irene to investigate further. It had begun to occur to them all that Anne might actually be the instrument that could unlock many of the secrets of the universe.

On December 8, 1959, Jim and Anne decided to try again. Anne slipped easily into a hypnotic trance and was once more experiencing the life of Antonius. "I'm fastened to a big wheel by my legs and neck," she moaned. "They're stretching me! They're tightening it. I can't stand it!" she screamed.

"Who's doing this to you?" Jim demanded to know. "Who is the man giving the orders?"

"Two slaves are pulling the wheel. They're filthy dirty and dressed in ragged clothes. A third man is telling them what to do. He's very different. His clothes are fancy. He keeps telling them to pull the wheel tighter and tighter."

"Tell me more about this fancy guy. Do you know him? Look at his face."

"No, no, no! I don't want to look. Oh! He's just given orders to tighten the wheel again. 'Again,' he says. 'Again!' I'm going to break in two." She paused a moment and then continued. "I've passed out, but he's telling them to throw water on me. It's so cold."

For a time Anne seemed to detach herself from Antonius' agony and was able to describe the scene objectively. "It's such an awful place, so dirty with filthy straw on the floor. I see a tiny window near the ceiling. It's dawn. They've been torturing me all night. Now they're trying to decide what to do with me."

"Look at 'Fancy Pants' giving the orders," Jim reminded her. "Who is he? Tell me everything about him. How is he dressed?"

"He's wearing leather sandals that tie around his legs."

"What else?"

"A white tunic and a red cape."

"What about his face?"

"He's wearing a metal helmet with a red plume."

"Look at his face. Who is he?"

"I can't look! I can't, I can't!" Anne began to sob hysterically.

"All right," Jim relented momentarily. "Let's go back to before all this happend. Where were you? What were you doing?"

"I'm going to a party," Anne explained obediently. "It's in a big building, like a palace—maybe it is a palace. The floor and columns are marble. There's a beautiful garden outside. A girl is coming up to me. I kiss her and we sit down together on a soft couch with a lot of pillows. She keeps stroking me and running her fingers through my hair. I don't care much for her."

"What's happening now?"

"A man has given me a glass of wine and I'm drinking it. He's smiling at me, almost smirking." Anne's hands went to her mouth as though holding a large goblet. She tilted her head back as if drinking and then handed the goblet back to some invisible person.

"I feel so funny," she exclaimed. "I think I'm drunk. I'm trying to get up from the couch. The girl is trying to help me, but I'm too drunk to make it. I can't get up! I feel terrible."

"I think you have a 2000-year-old hangover," Jim ventured. He placed a plastic bucket beside her. Anne vomited several times but still remained locked in a deep hypnotic trance, feeling every bit of Antonius' nausea.

Finally moving forward in time, Anne described Antonius leaving the party. After six attempts to mount his horse, the man is at last able to ride away from the palace. Antonius gallops through the sleeping city, the hoof beats reverberating on his aching head. "He is on his way home," Anne explained.

After entering the stable adjoining the house, Antonius is so overcome with weakness and nausea that he flings himself down on the rough straw-covered floor and lies there for a time totally exhausted.

"I keep thinking that I got drunk for a reason," Anne said at last. "It was done to me for some purpose, I'm sure it was. I feel as though I'd been drugged. Surely only one drink couldn't do this."

"Who gave you the drink?" Jim asked.

"I don't know. I think—I'm not sure."

At last Antonius rises from the floor and walks toward the house, but Anne sees his steps growing shorter and shorter. His movements are slow, almost reluctant. "I don't want to go in. There's death inside. I know there is. I can't do it. Don't make me do it," she pleaded.

"You must go in. You must face whatever there is to face. If you don't do it now, you'll have to do it later," Jim insisted.

"I can't. It's terrible, terrible! I'm afraid to look. It's tearing me apart. Don't make me," she begged.

"I'll help you. I'm going to count from one to ten. When I reach ten, you'll feel much calmer, more detached," Jim assured her. "You will be able to look about the room. One, two, three, four, five, six, seven, eight, nine, ten. Now go in and look around you. What do you see?"

"It's a simple house. Stone walls, handmade furniture." She paused a moment, her head moving slowly as though surveying the room. "The furniture is all broken. The room is a mess. Oh, my God!" Anne threw back her head and screamed in horror. "Oh, it's worse than being tortured. Everyone I love. They're all dead," she sobbed. "In the firelight I see the bodies of my brothers. They've all been stabbed to death. My mother is lying on the floor. Her throat has been slashed from ear to ear."

Anne cried for a few moments and then her manner seemed to change. "I feel this terrible anger. I want to kill. I must kill the ones responsible for this," she said through clenched teeth. "I feel insanely angry. My head is splitting. It only adds to my rage, to my desire for revenge."

Anne then saw herself as Antonius "riding like the wind" through the open countryside. In the distance is a fleeing horseman. Antonius seems to know that this is one of the assassins. He draws closer to the man and throws a spear at him. The lone figure falls to the ground. Antonius turns and rides back toward town in search of the others. It is early morning now. As he rides past an area of jagged cliffs, he is suddenly set upon by a group of men who have apparently been waiting in ambush.

Anne's arms began to flail about wildly as though fighting for her life. "Oh, they've knocked me down," she said. "They think I'm unconscious but I'm not. I'm listening to them, watching for a chance to get away. Now I'm running. I'm so tired and confused. My legs will hardly move. I don't know where to go. Where can I hide? I'm on a horse now, but they're chasing me. I'm so very tired.

They throw something at me and I fall to the ground. I try to crawl, to hide, but it's no use. They have me," Anne said at last, utter fatigue and helplessness in her voice.

"They've tied me," she continued the narrative. "We're riding back into town. I'm riding double, tied to someone. Now they're dragging me down a flight of stone stairs into a dark cell. They're tying me to a rack. My legs are being stretched. I think one of them is broken. I can feel the bone wiggling. It must have happened when I fell off the horse."

"What's happening now?"

"I'm being pulled, ooooh! It hurts so much," Anne whimpered pitifully. She began to pant. Her whole body had arched upward so that only her shoulders and heels were touching the couch. She screamed again and again.

"Who's doing this to you?" Jim asked.

"No, no, no," Anne pleaded. "Leave me alone."

"Tell me everything about the man. You've got to know about him. Who is he? What does he mean to you?" Jim's voice was loud, demanding. He would not allow her to evade him by slipping away into her own half-world of pain.

"He's the man who gave me the drink at the party," Anne admitted at last.

"Then he must have wanted you drugged, perhaps to get you out of the way so your family could be killed. But maybe there's more to it. Why would he do such a thing? What does he mean to you? Who is he?"

"I don't know. I don't know," Anne cried.

"Look at him," Jim ordered. "Tell me everything about him. How is he dressed? Describe him from the top of his head to the tip of his toes."

"Oh, they're pulling me tighter and tighter. It takes two of them because I'm so big."

"What's the fancy guy doing?"

"He's enjoying it."

"Tell me about him."

"He's wearing a helmet with a plume."

"What about his face. Tell me about his face."

"I can't, I can't."

"All right, describe his clothes again."

"A red cape, he's wearing a red cape. He's dark, not too tall. His eyes are blue."

"You do know him! Who is he? Tell me."

"I don't know. Oh, it can't be, it can't be!"

"Why can't it be? Who is it?"

"He looks like you! He is you!" Anne screamed at last and then broke into uncontrollable sobs. "It is you, it is you," she cried again and again.

"All right, all right. Move forward. Leave this scene," Jim urged with quiet firmness. "You know all that you need to know. Move on now."

Once again Anne was reliving the last terrible moments of Antonius' life. "Oh, my head!" she screamed as she felt the final agony of the man being dragged over the rough cobblestones. "They think I'm dead, but I'm not," she whispered, and then the screams came again and the sound of Antonius' throat filling with dust and blood. Finally there came the terrible sound of the man's death rattle.

To his horror, Jim realized that Anne had actually stopped breathing. "Breathe!" he commanded. "Breathe! Snap out of it," he cried, his voice rising in panic. "I'm going to count from five to one, then you will wake up. One, two, three, four, five. Awake!"

She did not respond and he quickly began to administer artificial respiration. Anne remained perfectly quiet. She was still not breathing. Jim was overcome with a sense of loss and remorse. He was certain that she was dead. "I've killed Anne by pushing her too far," he thought. Then Jim remembered the mouth-to-mouth resuscitation technique Anne had recently taught him and bent over her. Slowly, very slowly, she began to show signs of life until at last her breathing had returned to normal.

"It could have been a kind of psychic setup," Anne says today, recalling the experience after more than fifteen years. "I had only learned mouth-to-mouth resuscitation the week before. It was part of a first-aid course that I'd been required to take because I was a Girl Scout leader. Teaching Jim to do it was really a joke, something neither of us took seriously at the time. It's amazing that he even remembered what to do. We both feel that it was all meant to be. I simply was not supposed to die at that time. My purpose in this life had only just begun to manifest itself. At the same time, my almost dying may have been a kind of warning—a reminder to us both that the human spirit is encased in a fragile body that can only be pushed so far."

Neither Jim nor Anne seemed to feel a great deal of surprise that he had been her tormentor in a previous life. "Afterward, as we listened to the tape recording together, Jim admitted that he had somehow been expecting to be identified as 'Fancy Pants.' I felt as though I, too, had known all along but hadn't been ready to deal with it," Anne said.

"Now that the identity of Antonius' murderer was finally out in the open, both of us could place the event in its proper perspective. We could readily accept the fact that the death of Antonius had occurred a long time ago. We obviously were not the same people today that we were then. I had no sense of resentment toward Jim but I did have an inkling of karmic destiny. 'Fancy Pants' had manipulated Antonius on the rack. Jim, in a sense, was doing that to me in my present life. Though a kind, good man, he is very strong, very dominant. I realized suddenly what was happening between the two of us. Jim had been overpowering me. Now I knew without question that it was time for me to grow and to assert my own individuality.

"Jim had been a domineering interrogator, forcing me to face terrible things, but I had trusted his strength and his purpose. His judgment had been correct, but now I felt that there was much more to be learned and that I must push forward and assume personal responsibility. I was eager, no longer afraid."

These early experiences with hypnotic regression caused Anne to look back over her present lifetime and analyze the course it had taken. She had been born in Mexico, the child of a French father and a Spanish and French mother. A twin sister had died at birth. Her father had abandoned his wife prior to Anne's birth. In order to escape the domination of a family who shared the conviction of many Latins that a woman without a man is a kind of child-servant with no individual identity, Anne's mother remarried at the first opportunity.

"She was fearful that this might be her only chance to lead a life of her own," Anne explains. "I'm afraid that she regretted the decision all her life. She married and we came to the United States when I was a year and a half old. My stepfather was Greek and held a very old-country viewpoint regarding life in general. As a result, my home life in Texas and later in Glendale, California, was repressive—long on orthodox religion and short on everything else. We were very poor and, to make life even more difficult, my stepfather considered me an unwelcome reminder that my mother had known another man. He openly favored his own children, my half-brother and sister. I heard a lot about good and bad but I didn't have much faith in the source. As I grew up, I turned inward—searching for truth within myself. I was determined to achieve a richer life in every sense than what I had experienced thus far."

Anne was enterprising and independent. Upon graduating from high school, she worked her way through business college and became a legal stenographer. At twenty-one, she married Jim Armstrong, a man whom she had known for five years. "He was very strong, very protective," she recalls. "I felt a kind of closeness and understanding between us from the very beginning, a kind of instant affinity. For a long time it was enough to merely rely on his judgment. It was comforting after my childhood years of being so alone. Then, too, Jim's attitudes were very stimulating to me. His view of life was quite liberal and questioning, very different from the narrow, rigid thinking that I was accustomed to. He turned me on to many things, many new ideas.

"Not long after our marriage Jim was transferred to Farmington, Utah, a tiny town with very little in the way of cultural resources. I took advantage of the solitude to study philosophy. I was fascinated by theosophy and by the principles of the Rosicrucian Order. As my concepts broadened, I began to meditate. Then, without warning, I had the sensation of leaving my body. It was a terrifying experience, one that I simply could not handle. I gave up my mystical questing and stopped meditating entirely. There were no more out-of-body experiences, but the conflict going on inside me seemed to trigger more frequent reoccurrences of the fierce headaches that had plagued me sporadically since childhood.

"I tried to concentrate on just being a housewife. We moved to Sacramento and after a while our daughter, Christine, was born. I suppose you can say my life was pretty average. I occupied myself with the usual things, PTA, gardening, and all that; but, as the years passed, my headaches grew more and more severe. I tried all kinds of treatments and all kinds of doctors, but nothing worked until I met Irene Hickman. From then on, it seems my whole life changed. The Antonius experience and the gift of mediumship that developed afterward seemed to bring Jim and I closer than we had ever been. He was excited by the fact that I was able to see into the minds of others more and more frequently and could often warn them of approaching difficulties. He encouraged me to work with Irene but also enjoyed hypnotizing me himself. Since so many of the lives that were brought out under hypnosis included him as well, it seemed very clear to us both that we must literally be made for one another.

"Chris also appeared in many of these past-life memories. She has been my child more than once. Unfortunately Chris wasn't nearly so enthralled by my psychic transformation as Jim was. I suppose that it would be hard for any nine-year-old— Chris's age when all this began—to understand. She never knew when she came home from school just who I might be or what I'd be doing. It must all have seemed very strange and probably a little embarrassing. Children are pretty conventional when it comes to their parents. They want mother to be exactly like everyone else's mother. Now, of course, it's very different. She's well into her twenties and considers psychic research to be very in. It isn't easy to be a heroine in one's own family, but I may be approaching it."

As intrigued as Anne naturally was by the revelation of Antonius, she did not attempt to study Roman history. "Of course I was terribly interested," she admits, "but I didn't want to contaminate any of the information that was coming through. I didn't want my mind playing tricks on me in any way that I could consciously anticipate. I wouldn't even attend a movie about Rome.

"Then three years after the Antonius regression, my husband was given the NATO assignment of establishing French and Italian missile sites. As a result, we had the choice of living in either France or Rome for six months while he advised on the development of rocket propellants. The opportunity to really experience Rome—not just visit it fleetingly, which was all I'd ever dreamed of doing— seemed like a mystic gift.

"Following the Antonius experience I had begun to develop as a medium. Entities from the other side were able to use me as a kind of channel to relay information to living persons who needed it. I discovered that I could use this new ability to help others; but I hesitated sometimes, uncertain of the reality of what was happening. It was so far out, so contrary to what I'd been taught as a child. It seemed incredible that I could be right and so many really devout, well-meaning people wrong.

"Perhaps the trip to Rome was 'given' to me as a means of building my confidence so that I could grow as a medium. As I explored the ruins of the Forum and the Senate, I was able to see the city as Antonius had seen it, through his very eyes. One day while walking behind the Forum, I came upon the statue of a man. It was perfect except for the head, which was missing. Instinctively I fell to the ground before the marble form. 'Master,' I said, as though in loving supplication. Then abruptly I regained awareness of myself as Anne Armstrong kneeling on the ground before a headless statue and got up with some embarrassment.

"'Who is that?' I asked the guide.

"'Julius Caesar,' he replied.

"Suddenly I was overcome with a sense of love and adoration for Caesar. I knew then with an unquestionable certainty that Caesar was the man with the gold wreath that I had seen under hypnosis. I had an overwhelming sense of having failed this wonderful man who had been so good to me. Scenes of the many kind and wonderful things that he had done for me seemed to flood my mind. He had taken me from nothing and raised me to a place of authority and esteem. I had been his protégé. While walking about the Circus Maximus, I experienced a sense of intense excitement. I was certain that as Antonius I had performed there and won many prizes. I could see Antonius riding his chariot down the Appian Way and I compared that triumphant figure returning victorious from the games with the broken body tied to the rack. How tragic it all seemed, how wasteful. I felt such utter futility.

"As I walked about the ancient ruins, memories returned to me, filling in the gaps in the Antonius story. The why of it all was suddenly painfully clear. I had been approached by 'Fancy Pants' and the others who were planning to overthrow Caesar because they knew that I was very close to the ruler. I could have been of great help to them and would have been richly rewarded, but I angrily refused. Caesar was my god! Instead of aiding the plotters I had tried repeatedly to warn Caesar of what was going on, but he seemed strangely unconcerned. It was as though he had felt a premonition of the future but would not—or could not—alter his course to avoid assassination.

"I think now that he must have sensed an inevitability about it all. Perhaps he felt that destiny was propelling him forward along a predestined course and that he as an individual could not change history. As a mere man he had no choice but to play out the role assigned him. I—as Antonius—was impatient with this fatalism. With all the vigorous idealism of youth, I adored Caesar and could not bear to see him so oblivious to a danger that I knew to be very real. I was determined to change his destiny. I knew the enemy plan and rallied support among my friends. When the enemy attempted to move in on Caesar at the Senate, we would close ranks and protect him and then counterattack, killing them all. Surely no one else would dare to try such a thing again. Caesar would at last be safe.

"Having tried so many times before to caution Caesar, I felt that one more warning would mean nothing. I was certain that he would refuse to deviate from his course. It would be useless to attempt to persuade him to remain away from the Senate, to stay within the safety of the palace. I was sure that the only way to save him was a counterattack during the assassination attempt itself. My plan might very well have worked, but I never had an opportunity to put it into effect. I was far too confident, too sure of my own ability. The traitors had warned me that if I didn't join them I would be killed along with everyone that I held dear. The idea had seemed absurd to me. I was so young and strong, it never occurred to me for a minute that I would be unable to protect myself and my beloved Caesar. I had laughed at 'Fancy Pants,' who was as one with Brutus.

"Could the course of history have been changed if Antonius had been more prudent? That's a question that I've asked myself many times. If Antonius had not gone to the party, had not allowed himself to be tricked .... He died before the murder of Caesar knowing that he had failed, but without divulging the names of any of his friends who were aware of some of the details of the counterplot. I could feel every bit of the desperation and misery of Antonius, could sense his crumbling arrogance.

"Walking about the ruins, I could recall the strength and the magnificence that was Rome. I could hear the clatter of chariots on the cobblestones and the slap of sandaled feet on the cool marble floors. The hatred and the violence and the love were ashes now and a part of me as well. It all means nothing today, just a few paragraphs in a history book, but I can still feel the loyalty and the love for that man who represented so much to me. And I can still see and feel the body of Antonius, the muscle and the strength, the handsome, smiling face, the careless confidence. It's very real. It all happened to me. I have no doubt of that."

Although it was the discovery of Antonius that triggered Anne's mediumship, he is not the only past-life memory recalled under hypnosis. Working with Irene Hickman, Anne was plunged first into the existence of a colonial thief whose life came to an abrupt end when he attempted to steal a man's watch, and then into the body of a hermaphrodite embalmed alive during ancient times.

"I'm sure that I recalled both of those existences for a purpose," Anne says. "The thief incarnation came to me when Irene was asking some very probing questions regarding my sense of will, my tendency to hold on to things—particularly material things. All of a sudden I experienced a choking sensation that was quite frustrating. Irene suspected possible karmic implications and asked, 'When did you feel like this before?'

"I felt a bursting sensation in my throat and lungs as though they were filling with water. When I haltingly explained this to Irene, she suggested that I detach myself from the situation immediately, but that I attempt to observe objectively what was happening and describe it to her. I relaxed a bit and kind of stood off, watching. In one sense it was all happening to me, but in another sense I was merely seeing a very vivid picture, like a movie. I saw myself lying face down in a muddy pool. I was a man, dark-skinned and clad in ragged clothing. A dagger lodged between my shoulder blades had hit a nerve, paralyzing me so that I couldn't move my head or arms. Instinctively I gasped for breath, taking in huge gulps of water each time. I could feel my lungs fill until it seemed that they would explode. I was sinking down further and further into the murky water. At last I came to rest on the bottom. I felt very comfortable now, very relaxed. Death had come and I was slipping out of my body."

Going back to the minutes just prior to the entity's drowning, Anne recalled a tremendous struggle between herself and another man. "He claims that I stole something from him," she explained.

"Did you?" Irene probed.

"Yes, a very big beautiful watch. I see it clearly. It has rubies all around the face. I stole it from the other man while he was standing in a crowd. I had no rules or moral laws to live by. I wanted the watch so I took it."

"You couldn't have been a very good pickpocket to get caught like that."

"Pickpocketing was only a sideline for me. I had a ship anchored just offshore of which I was very proud. I thought it was beautiful. I must have been a pirate because the ship was full of things I'd stolen. I should have left well enough alone, been satisfied with what I had; but obviously I was greedy. I didn't realize when the elegantly dressed man took the watch out of his pocket that it was attached to his buttonhole. I just grabbed it and ran. The man chased me.

He apparently had a small dagger inside his coat pocket. It hit me right between the shoulder blades and I fell into the pool. I took the watch down with me and died with it clenched in my fist. Later when my body floated upward, my hand relaxed but the watch sank to the bottom. It's still there. It didn't do anyone any good."

In evaluating the experience, Anne felt that it was related to her very human tendency to hold on to things. "Perhaps this life was revealed to me as a kind of lesson that, in the final reality, material things have very little importance," she ventured.

Another equally relevant reminder came to Anne, again under hypnosis, when she recalled being mummified. "Oh, it's terrible, just terrible," she told Dr. Hickman.

"Let's go back to the time before you became a mummy and talk about the life leading up to this experience," Irene suggested.

"The body was preserved before it was dead."

"How did they do that? Detach yourself completely and describe it to me."

"They used tubes. They inserted tubes into my body. Tubes went into my nostrils and under my arms. Then this terrible fluid was pumped into my body."

"Is this a ritual of some kind or is it done to everyone who is near death?"

"No, it was done specially to me. Being embalmed alive is a very sacred process. It's a privilege, really an honor."

"How did you come by this honor?"

"I can't tell if I'm a man or a woman! It has something to do with that. This is a very confused feeling. I don't like it."

"Perhaps you are neither. Is that possible?"

"I don't think I am. No, no, I'm not. The people carry me everywhere because I'm so special—that is, they *think* I'm so special. I wear only silk robes and my feet never touch the ground. The people believe that I am pure because I have the attributes of the female and those of the male so perfectly balanced."

"If you were so perfect in that existence, why are you back in the world now?"

"I wasn't perfect at all—not emotionally or spiritually. People just thought I was. My face was very, very smooth and my hair was soft and curly. I was built like a small man but, yet I had this beautiful hair and lovely facial features. My breasts were more developed than a man's and my fingers were long and beautiful. People came from everywhere to admire me. They thought that I was divine, but I knew that this was all wrong."

"You really had a good racket going."

"Yes, that's true; but it didn't make me very happy. I was living a lie, being honored for nothing more than an accident of nature. I wasn't really balanced at all. I was simply trapped in a crazy mixed-up body. I hated this deception. Then, when I was only twenty-five, I became paralyzed. It started in my spine and when it reached my head the people decided that I would be embalmed alive as a special honor. They wanted to preserve forever my 'perfect' body."

"Were you willing or unwilling to undergo this ordeal?"

"I was willing, eager really. Oddly enough I was happy that it would soon be over, that the lie would die with me. The people built a beautiful tomb for me. It still exists. It's near Egypt, but not in Egypt. It will be found one day."

"It would appear that since you recall the mummification process so vividly, it must have some important significance for you," Dr. Hickman said. "Do you have any idea what it might be?"

"Yes, yes, I think I do," Anne said slowly, as though pondering the scene before her. "Because of the embalming technique, the body was preserved for a very long time; and, as long as it didn't completely deteriorate, a part of my spirit was locked inside, forced to remain with the mummy. This was not a very pleasant experience—being tied to that dreadful body. Bondage to any body after death is bad enough, but this was particularly awful, to remain chained to the tragic freak of nature that had been my prison in life."

"Is this what happens to others that are mummified—are they also confined to their bodies?"

"Yes, burial also impedes spiritual progress, but it's not as bad as being mummified. Thank goodness no one is doing that any more. Cremation is best. The body is destroyed right away, freeing the spirit to go on its way."

Anne feels that her long attachment to the body of the hermaphrodite has a very real implication for her present life. "Because I developed the gift of mediumship, others in this lifetime might begin to think of me as something special when I'm not at all. I've merely taken certain qualities that we all have and developed them in a slightly different pattern; but it's a pattern that others can use as well, a pattern that we all carry within ourselves. Perhaps the memory was sent to me to make certain that I don't allow some kind of cult to form about myself, that I continue to use my mediumship as a cultivated gift to enrich and aid others and not as an ego trip for my own gratification."

Still other past lives revealed themselves when Jim hypnotized Anne. Once he succeeded in regressing her so far that she reached a prehistoric form. "Are you a man or a woman?" he asked.

"I don't know," she replied in bewilderment. "I'm so hairy that I can't tell."

In this life Anne saw scenes of herself scavenging for survival. "Once I was slurping the insides out of a very large egg. It looked pretty awful by today's standards, but I certainly seemed to be enjoying it," she recalls.

On January 10, 1960, Anne was regressed to a life in Palestine. This time she saw herself entering a small hut, a jug balanced on her head. "I'm a woman, about twenty years old," she said. "I'm wearing a long handwoven tunic with a sash and a cross about my throat, which I tuck inside my clothing. When I think of the cross, I'm frightened. There are two cute little boys inside. They're my children and they seem to be waiting for me to fix their breakfast."

"Do either of the boys remind you of anyone?" Jim asked.

"Of course, what's the matter with me! Why didn't I realize right away? It's Chris, but she's a boy in this life. She's a little boy about four years old. The other boy is probably seven. I don't recognize him. They're both so dear, but I'm frightened for them. I'm almost afraid to look at them. I can sense that something terrible is going to happen to us all."

"What are you afraid of?"

"It has to do with our religion. Our faith means everything to us, but we always have to hide. So far we have been able to keep our meetings a secret, but some day we'll be discovered. It's impossible to hide anything for long. Oh, I just know I won't have the children very much longer. There are very important people who come through town, very rich people with armor and fine clothes and lavish chariots. They whip us, take what little we have, and knock our children down. Our religion tells us that we must not hate them, but it's hard not to. They are so cruel, so arrogant.

"Now I'm in another place," Anne continued. "The buildings are much grander. The countryside seems greener. My husband, who is a shepherd, says it would be a good place to raise sheep. We're in a huge building. There are many tiny cells underground and that's where we are chained. Parties and feasts are taking place upstairs. The people just use us for entertainment. Everybody sits there eating and drinking and laughing while the lions eat us! Oh, I can't watch this, I can't! The lions! Oh, it's just horrible, horrible."

Jim did not allow Anne to linger in this state, recalling their previous near-disaster. Instead he regressed her even farther back in time. In this life Anne discovered herself living with Jim as her husband on the continent of Atlantis. Jim was a simple stonecutter who longed to design great buildings but lacked the education. Despite his dreams, he was not unhappy with the menial tasks assigned him and worked diligently. In this life Chris was again their child, a daughter. The family was able to escape as Atlantis became inundated with water. Jim was one of the few who believed that a holocaust was coming. As the water rose higher and higher, he built a small boat that sustained them for a time; but eventually they, too, were drowned when the boat capsized.

"Jim and I were together in yet another life," Anne says. "This time I was a temple dancer in Arabia. Jim was a priest in the same temple. Our lives were dedicated to the deity and we were forbidden to think of sex or even romantic love. All who resided in the temple were expected to remain celibate in mind as well as body. Jim disobeyed this order. He fell deeply in love with me against his will and even though I did nothing to encourage him. Others eventually found out about this terrible breach of faith. Jim felt such great remorse at his inability to control his emotions and at the disgrace he had brought upon himself that he committed suicide. He was only twenty-two. I died a few years later of a heart attack while dancing in the temple. I was eighteen at the time. As I watched my body being carried in a funeral procession I became aware of Jim's spirit beside me. He had been waiting for me. I must confess my reaction was, 'Oh, no, not you again!' It seemed that he had been pursuing me through all eternity and perhaps he has."

Still another part of the grand design was a brief life as

a boy in Scotland who appeared to live in a castle. "I think my name was Christopher," Anne says. "I see 'us' riding horses and playing with pet swans. Christopher had a kindly older friend who was a shepherd and a very pretty mother. His life seemed to start out well enough, but it ended so soon. In the final scene of his existence I see him standing on a high cliff overlooking the sea when somehow he seems to have lost his footing. In that regression I was quite objective; I felt pity as I watched the boyish figure wearing a bright plaid kilt hurtle through the air, but no great involvement. What a shame, though, Christopher was only thirteen when he died."

Jim was rather disconcerted by Anne's numerous tragic existences. "Didn't you *ever* have a pleasant life and an easy death?" he asked at last. They decided to go back and find out.

After being placed in a deep hypnotic trance, Anne sat silently for a time, her hands engaged in a series of intricate movements. "I'm a temple dancer," she announced at last and began to move lightly about the room as though keeping time to a rhythm heard only by herself. The dance was solemn, ritualized, slow, and graceful. Anne concluded her movements in a kneeling position, hands folded, her head down.

"Are you in Arabia?" Jim asked.

"No, Siam. My name is Merijah."

"What are you wearing, Merijah?"

"A gold cap with a kind of spire on it, a tight-fitting gold blouse and filmy pants. My sandals are pointed and I'm wearing many gold bracelets. I have long fingernails."

Moving forward in time, she saw herself awakening in a very big bed.

"Who shares the bed with you?" Jim asked.

"The fat man."

"Who is the fat man?"

"He's very important."

"How old is he?"

"Forty."

"How old are you?"

"Eighteen."

Merijah went on to describe the luxurious palace where she lived, a white marble building with three large domes. Several other girls shared the same wing of the palace, but they did not occupy the bed of the fat man on a regular basis as she apparently did. "We don't do much, just talk a lot and laugh. I dance and play an instrument with strings," she said.

"What are you doing now?"

"Getting up. It's morning."

"What are you wearing?"

"Not much. He likes it better that way." Anne sat down before an imaginary dressing table and surveyed herself. "I have long black hair. I'm quite dark and have greenish slanted eyes. I'm oriental-looking, very small, and slender. I have nice hands."

"Who taught you to dance?"

"A very special teacher here at the palace."

"All right, now go through a regular day and tell me all about it," Jim directed.

"I have breakfast with the other girls. It's mostly fruit, dark bread, and milk. There are ten of us sitting at the table, some slightly older than myself, others a little younger. We chatter a lot. An old lady sits at the head of the table. She sees to it that we have everything that we want. Now I'm going back to my room to get dressed. I have lots of clothes. He buys them for me. The other girls don't have as many as I do. The fat man is very rich. He doesn't seem to work. I have someone to help me dress— the other girls don't. My maid is a girl a little older than I. She's putting perfume all over me. My dress is blue, embroidered in gold. I wear gold sandals. I don't like the fat man too well, but he's kind to me, and the life at the palace is much better than life on the outside. I was poor before I came here. I love to dance. I see myself dancing and bowing before a great stone Buddha. It's an honor to dance in the temple. I am very lucky to be chosen for such an honor. I dance often at important affairs. There isn't much else to tell about. I talk and giggle a lot with the other girls. I please the fat man and he gives me many pretty things."

"Go forward then. Tell me where Merijah is at the age of thirty," he instructed.

"I'm crippled. I can hardly walk and my mind—well, it's funny. I can't think very well. I can't seem to reason. I think maybe I'm crazy but it doesn't seem to bother me."

"Where are you?"

"I think I may be in the same palace, but not the same room. I'm comfortable, but it isn't as luxurious as the other place. I seem to have everything I need. People take care of me. I'm not alone."

"Go forward to two weeks prior to the time of your death. How old are you?"

"Thirty-one."

"Go forward to your death. Don't experience it, just tell me about it. You will watch yourself and your surroundings as though through a television screen. Look at Merijah. How did she die?"

"She—why, she had syphilis! I guess she got it from the fat man, but apparently it didn't affect him as badly. He saw to it that she was well taken care of. It seems that one of the other girls first noticed the symptoms when Merijah was about twenty. She had to stop dancing at the temple and that saddened her, but not for long. Her mind began to deteriorate quite rapidly and she was too confused to even realize how crippled she had become. She looks like an old woman, but was not particularly uncomfortable or unhappy. I don't think she knew what was going on. It was a peaceful death. She just went to sleep in the afternoon and never woke up."

"How do you feel?"

"Wonderful," Anne said, stretching. "It's nice to be

free of that crippled body. I can see Merijah being cre-
mated."

"Do you feel any remorse about dying or any emotion
at watching the body—your body—being burned? Do you
have any sense of pain?"

"None at all. I can see the muscle reflexes causing the
body to jump as it burns. She's contorting now, rearing
back. Her hair and clothes are on fire. It's a strange
sensation to watch, but I don't feel any pain. I can feel the
warmth from the fire, but it doesn't burn me. Now she's
been reduced to ashes. It's all over; people are walking
away. The spirit of Merijah simply took off as soon as she
died without even a backward glance. She had no regrets
and was clearly ready to move on to some other experience."

Through many such hypnotic sessions a vast mosaic of
past life experiences began to take form with an instinctive
set of balances and counterbalances. After a rather giddy,
aimless life as the amatory attraction in a Siamese harem,
Anne believes that she was reborn as Gilbert Sorenson, a
Puritan colonist in the eastern United States.

"After I ceased to be Merijah I had a sense of scanning
the entire world looking for a place to be born again. I'd
had a restful life and was ready to be on to something else,
somebody else," she explained. "It seemed as though there
were millions of people below me. Then I picked out
where I wanted to be. It was strange to be a baby again. I
was so tiny, so helpless."

Anne recalled growing up in a rough log cabin and, as
a young man, being wounded in an Indian attack. She felt
intensely the pain of having the arrow wound cauterized,
but knew that Gilbert Sorenson recovered and lived a long
life.

"I really didn't care to pursue this one," Anne laughs
today. "I had enough religious repression in my present
lifetime. The Catholics and the Calvinists who wasted so

much time fighting and killing each other would be amazed at how much they have in common—mostly things I'm striving to evolve beyond this time around."

Anne believes that all humans return again and again to earth in different bodies, different countries, different periods in history in order to learn new truths. "Each life teaches us some new lesson, adds some fresh kernel of wisdom. I believe the ultimate goal is the achievement of a perfect balance of yin and yang within ourselves—the positive and the negative, the spiritual and the physical, the masculine and the feminine—no, not in the manner of the poor hermaphrodite who was merely an average person trapped in an unnatural body, but a totally balanced spirit."

She perceives the cosmos as a great pond where each entity swims as a tiny polliwog. "Each polliwog has some slight individualization but is only a fragment of the universal pool," she says. "Each entity has a mission and must leave the pond from time to time to pursue his destiny. Yet we always remain attached to our essential core, as an embryo is fastened to its umbilical cord. When our life on earth has ended, we return with fresh awareness to our original source.

"The mind becomes the vehicle through which we change and express our destiny, but the central core remains the same. The pond is the sea of life. The polliwogs are part of the same energy assuming different forms. Part of the pain of life is knowing that there is something more. Always there is a mystic tie to that original source, pulling us back. All of us have a divine spark within us, a mass of pure energy which we clothe in many forms. This seething mass of energy constantly seeks awareness and form, but the form is merely an illusion. The yin and yang within us all is a drive to experience from every point of view. Our final mission is to become one with the godhead.

"I can now go back in memory to the very beginning of time when the earth was a molten mass waiting to receive life. As the earth cooled, bits of consciousness became

individualized. At that time there was no difference between God and ourselves. Then, as we began to move out
through the various stages of consciousness, we took on
substance. Though the central core of our existence has
never changed and will never change, each offshoot of this
essential being has a lesson to be learned. One of the most
difficult of these lessons is that of independence. All of us
must learn that—though we are born into a family unit—
we are not really a part of that family. We have merely
placed ourselves in a necessary environment for some form
of inner growth. Individual relationships are transitory
things. Each of us must learn to function as a separate
entity.

"I—like everyone else alive today—chose this current
existence, these present circumstances, in order to gain
knowledge and ultimate fulfillment. In this life I now know
that my destiny is to use the powers of mediumship for the
welfare of others.

"A variety of experiences are required for us all and
each has a special part to play in our inevitable development. Pampering and indulgence may be a very necessary
thing for an individual at one point in time. The Merijah
existence must have been a kind of vacation after all I'd
previously endured and so was essential at that particular
level of experience. But now it is necessary for me to learn
self-reliance, to think and develop as a strong individualist.
This is necessary for any medium; there can be no reaching
out to others. Knowledge and confidence must come from
within."

Anne admits that lifetime tasks are not easy to fulfill.
"Sometimes we overplan," she says. "We're very brave in
the world beyond. We think that we can do anything when
we return to earth. We forget what it's like down here. Up
there our senses are dulled to the physical existence just as
down here they are dulled to the spiritual. It all looks so
simple. We lay out an intricate life pattern for ourselves
and think there's nothing to following it. 'Of course, I can

do it,' we say. But once we're placed in the actual situation, life has a way of tumbling in on us.

"I was very ambitious. I was certain that I could get everything out of the way this trip. I thought I could take anything that came my way—after all, think of what I'd already experienced! Fortunately our bodies have a way of warning us when we're rushing too fast, not approaching problems in a steady, measured way. When physical breakdowns occur, they're really a means of protecting us from ourselves. A physical problem enables our subconscious to shut a few doors, to relax a little and go at things properly. But sometimes we don't heed the signs; we try to ignore the headaches or whatever. We plunge headlong into work that's too much for us. We feel driven by some inner need that is rarely understood. All we know is that we must hurry, must work harder.

"Such haste really isn't necessary and often defeats its own purpose. At the end of each lifetime we check off the things that we have done and learned. This balance is carried forward to the next page or lifetime and all that we have learned can be incorporated into the next existence. There is really no need to make life miserable for ourselves by rushing. It's far better to get a few jobs accomplished in the right way than to attempt too many things in a haphazard fashion. That's really a tremendous lesson—one that I'm only now learning. The essentials are waiting for our careful, thoughtful attention. The many electives will take care of themselves at the proper time.

"In the past when I found things to be very difficult, when doors seemed to be closed, I only tried all the harder. I should have realized that the very difficulty was an indication that I should abandon these tasks for the time being and turn to other things. The lifetime chores that are meant for us are rarely difficult. A talent, a gift is always there waiting to be uncovered and utilized in a manner beneficial to ourselves and others. My job in this life is to learn to understand myself and my relationship to other people. My required course is to help others through my mediumship. People seek me out and it seems very natural that I should help them with the psychic insights that I receive. But if I attempted to be all things to all people I would lose touch with the one gift that makes me unique. This is true one way or another with all of us."

Anne at first was frightened by her developing powers to see into the minds of others and to make predictions. "I was terribly worried, afraid that I might misuse this gift in some way. I knew that there was something significant buried beyond the Antonius existence and suspected some dark secret. I feared that evil in some way lay behind my growing ability to see into the minds of others and predict the future or recall the past. Did I dare unleash a strength that I could not fully comprehend?"

In an effort to find the cause of her hidden fears, Anne asked Dr. Hickman to regress her beyond the life of Antonius to the beginning of the karma that had resulted in his violent death. As she sank deeper and deeper into a hypnotic trance, Anne saw herself on a high parapet looking down at hundreds of people.

"I am very powerful," she said. "These people bow before me out of fear. I have dominion over many things, including the life and death of my subjects; but it's much bigger than that. I have supernatural powers as well. I had begun to develop these powers in yet another life, a still earlier existence, but then died before I could really use them to advantage. I was so anxious to hurry back in order that I could experience this gift more fully. I intended to use it for good, but somehow I got mixed up. I had received my occult powers too quickly. There was no time to fully understand what was happening or to evaluate myself—my strengths and my weaknesses—objectively. I feel an outside influence as well. Someone persuaded me very early to misuse my gift, but obviously I was quite willing to be persuaded. Anyway, despite my good intentions, I got off on the wrong foot almost from the begin-

ning. If you are weak and then get a taste of power, you
don't want to lose it. That power became my security and
my obsession.

"There is a heavy ring that I like to wear, a moonstone
ring. I can stare into it and see visions that come true. *I can
make them come true.* I see myself sitting on a great carved
chair. I am very beautiful, tall and slender. My gown—
what there is of it—is very elegant. My breasts are bare
and my nipples are painted red to match my filmy skirt.
I'm very proud of my regal appearance. Jim is with me in
this life. He is my slave. He loves me, but disapproves of
my life. He tries to tell me that I am evil and must change
for my own good. He says that I am hurting myself more
than anyone else but I refuse to listen. In a way I love and
hate him at the same time. I don't like the things he tells
me because they cause me to question the prerogatives
that I've come to take for granted. I'm hooked on the
power, the excitement. I won't give that up merely for a
slave's pious chatter. It infuriates me that Jim—a mere
slave—should actually refuse to make love to me. I make
him attend all kinds of wild parties. They're orgies, really,
with no holds barred. I make him watch everything, every
kind of depravity. When he tries to preach to me, I have
him whipped. He's not afraid of me, no matter what I do.
Nothing discourages him from trying to persuade me to
change my life.

"As the time passes I see myself growing more and
more evil. My marriage has been one of convenience and
alliance. My husband comes to bore me, so I secretly have
him killed. Now I am in complete control. I can do
anything I please. I have become totally wanton and delight in ordering human sacrifices. It becomes a kind of
ritual done for my enjoyment and that of my guests. The
victims are placed in large basins; then their juglar veins
are cut. The blood—the life—drains out of them as we
watch eagerly. It's very amusing; some die quickly while
others take hours. The blood is then gathered in chalices

and placed at the feet of hideous idols. I watch hundreds of these sacrifices and delight in each because it is I who decides who the victim will be.

"I rule by fear alone for I am able to perform tremendous feats of occult strength. I can command fire into being at will and I can cause an unfortunate subject to literally freeze to death. I do this merely to satisfy a whim on my part. I can create whatever I please, ugly winged creatures or great slithering snakes. The power that I now have to heal I used then to destroy.

"The only one who seems immune to my black arts is Jim. He remains unyielding and unafraid. I can't seem to touch him. I try to use my power on him and he merely stands there, looking so sad as though he actually pities *me*! This is infuriating, not to be borne! Then one night he refuses me once too often and I determine to destroy him forever. I see it all so clearly. A large party is going on. People are laughing and drinking, pursuing every vile proclivity imaginable. I am wearing lavish gold jewelry, many bracelets, and a heavy gold necklace. This time my nipples are painted green to match a diaphanous skirt of emerald green. My eyeshadow and fingernails are green as well. I'm twenty-five now, at the height of my powers— very strong, very beautiful. Poor Jim seems so young. He is only eighteen but he has a strength of his own. It enables him to defy me. He will not yield to my desires. I have him carried into the banquet room tied to a huge golden platter. Then I pick up a golden spike and drive it through his head. It enters just below his right ear and goes straight through and out the other side."

Anne paused in her narrative, hands covering her face as she sobbed. "Oh, my God! How could I have done it? No wonder I have such terrible headaches. I'm feeling his pain.

"Poor Jim," she continued once more, absorbed in the tragic vision before her eyes. "It's so awful. It's the cruelest method that I can devise. The pain is excruciating and it takes him a long time to die. I am curiously lonely without him. It is easy to find willing slaves—male and female— with none of Jim's scruples. I don't lack for diversion as the years pass. Every wish is gratified. Then a crippling disease strikes me. I watch in horror as my beautiful body slowly begins to shrivel. My occult powers are suddenly useless. I cannot save myself from this relentless affliction. I don't want to go on living looking as do. I hate myself as I am now. I was so proud of my tall, supple body; now I don't want anyone to see me. It's too humiliating. People may actually be laughing at me or even pitying me.

"Suicide seems the only escape from my misery. I think about it carefully, weighing the various means of killing myself. Finally I order a female slave to clothe me in my most costly gown. She dresses my hair in an elaborate style. I command her to bring me a glass of wine and then dismiss her after giving orders that the building should be set on fire. I am determined that no one shall look again on my ugly, twisted shape. I'm alone now, leaning back against the scarlet pillows of my silken couch. I open the moonstone ring and sprinkle some powder from a secret compartment into the wine. It smells slightly of almonds. I watch fascinated as the powder slowly dissolves. Soon I'll be free of this hideous body. I'm a little afraid, reluctant to relinquish my great power, but it seems that I have no choice. I'm tired and weak, exhausted from a life of total abandon. I can't go on any longer. I drink the wine and the glass falls to the floor. My body is becoming paralyzed. It begins at the back of my neck and then travels down my shoulders, down my legs. I'm frightened now, I'm fighting death. I'm afraid to leave my body. The room is on fire. I'm burning but I don't want to die. I've killed so many and now it's my turn and I'm afraid to go.

"Suddenly I see my former slave standing nearby. He's come to help me. I don't understand it. How could anyone want to help after the terrible thing that I did to him? He's taking me by the hand. I'm out of the body now and he's leading me. I'm looking back at my body. It's so ugly, so contorted. He says that my life here is over now and I have a new chance, that I don't have to be that way again if I am willing to understand what I've done and accept the consequences. He can only go so far with me. He has other work to do and cannot change what I have done in the past. He's leaving now. I'm all alone."

Anne now believes that she was allowed to expiate some of her sins by undergoing a kind of hell which she was able to recall quite vividly while under hypnosis. "I had a choice, you see," she explains today. "Hell isn't a compulsory thing; it's an alternative. We can come back to earth immediately and suffer through many lifetimes of torment or we can get some of our worst karma out of the way in the afterlife. The pain is much keener there, more intense; but it does eliminate so many, many lifetimes of agony down here. This was explained to me very carefully, very gently. I was told that I didn't have to endure it all at once if I didn't want to. There is always a choice: in life or in afterlife. I could either return to earth and experience many difficult existences or I could enter a kind of mystic valley where much of the damage that I had done could be expiated at one time.

"I chose to enter the valley—which is in every sense the valley of the shadow of death. I felt so small, so alone as I walked into that fearful place. It was very dark and the atmosphere was clammy and hot. Sometimes I was submerged in a thick boiling substance. (When people speak of hell and the smell of sulphur, it's no myth.) It seemed that I spent an eternity in those boiling vats. I couldn't breathe, I was choking. It was terrifying. I felt cut off from everything. I was totally helpless, remembering how I had once possessed vast power and used it merely to control others. Sometimes I could see the people that I had once tormented and was required to watch again as they suffered. Of course this time my feelings were very different for it was not enough that I merely watch while others were tortured. I had to actually *be* them and to relive every bit of their agony myself. I'd killed so many that this part of my ordeal seemed endless.

"There were other things as well. The monsters that I had once created at will to terrify others into submission were all about me. I could feel the snakes crawling over me in the dark and everywhere I looked I could see fearsome red eyes watching me endlessly. I was surrounded by horror. It was terrible, terrible. I was so frightened, so completely helpless, remembering always the power I had once possessed and then misused. There was nothing that I could do to help myself. All I could do was accept the horrible justice of it all. Yet after a time I became aware of a tiny spark within me and gradually I came to have faith that this little light would expand and illuminate my way. As time passed—centuries it seemed—the spark did grow bigger and bigger until it came to fill my entire being. Finally it seemed that the tiny spot within me had grown until it lit up the entire valley. Suddenly I found that the place that had seemed so fearsome was really very beautiful.

"I realized then that we all pass through the valley after death. Whether it is beautiful or ugly depends upon the amount of light that each of us takes inside with us as a result of our life on earth. Those who can't make it through the valley, those who give up and slip back to where they started, will immediately return to life only to be plunged into the same situations. Their lives on earth will be miserable existences; they are certain to be murdered or to die in some other gruesome fashion. There is no escape. It all remains to be worked out through one means or another, a lonely burden that no one else can lighten. But for the others—the ones who carry illumination with them—the valley can be a place of wonder and delight."

Anne feels that as a result of her searching via hypnosis she has been freed from the ties of the past. "It might otherwise have taken me lifetimes to draw it all together," she says now. "Finding out who I was, where I'd been, was a tremendous relief. It was like releasing a great burden. I felt very free, but at the same time a little lonely for I know now that I *am* truly alone—as we all are. No one but me is responsible for my actions. There is no use blaming anyone for anything. In the last analysis, we choose alone and we suffer or rejoice alone.

"Every life that I have recalled—even the tiny fragments of memories that most were—makes up the sum total of me, the person that I am today. I can draw from any or all of them as I choose. To delve any farther would be unnecessary at this juncture and may remain so throughout this lifetime. I am certain that my past lives were shown to me for a purpose and I feel that I am fulfilling that purpose now.

"Of all the entities revealed to me, the important ones are Antonius, Merijah, and the Black Priestess because the person I am today is a blending of those three personalities. Antonius was the epitome of strong, arrogant masculinity; and, at the opposite extreme, who could be more utterly feminine than Merijah? A pretty, sexy girl with nothing more to do than please one enamored man, she was the perfect counterpart to the Antonius incarnation—a classic example of the yin and yang principles that strive for balance in us all.

"The Black Priestess—the woman with the power—is almost a composite of the two. It was essential that I find and accept this spiritual ancestor whose heritage is the talent that I possess today.

"The instinctive knowledge of this savage creature with her dark power held me back for years—who knows, perhaps for lifetimes. It's natural enough that I would be wary of using the gifts that I sensed were locked within me. I was reluctant to do the things I knew I was capable of doing for fear of making a wrong move or saying a wrong word that might cause pain to someone else. It would be strange if I hadn't been cautious, considering the terrible hurt that I had caused so many. But having relived the Black Priestess' final ordeal, I have recalled her lesson as well. Now I realize that it is possible for me to draw from that reserve of power but still use it for good.

"In the interim existence after the Black Priestess had emerged from the valley, she elected to work with troubled spirits who had only just crossed over. In an effort to ease their path, she studied long and diligently. After a time she knew instinctively how these entities felt merely by looking at them. Now I, too, have this gift. That is why I am able to contact mentally those who have crossed over as well as human beings here on earth. I'm a kind of bridge between the two worlds. This is where I belong in the current existence.

"I see the Black Priestess, Antonius, and Merijah as the basic components that make this possible. Getting to know them was a means of getting in touch with myself, of drawing on past strengths and experiences in order to fortify myself as I am now. None of the memories came easily. I worked for weeks and weeks with Irene and Jim, struggling to recall a single significant episode. Each was hidden behind so many ancient fears. The whole recovery project took more than two years."

As Anne began to integrate the forces of the past, her clairvoyant abilities began to surface more and more frequently. "In the beginning I had a spirit guide who would tell me things," she recalls today. "He was a beautiful Hindu and I felt quite safe with him there. If he gave me a message for someone, I was very certain that it was good, safe information. Then one day he disappeared. I went to ask a question and he simply wasn't there.

"This was a shattering experience," she admits. "I really fell apart. The sense of failure was dreadful. I was sure that he was gone because I'd done something wrong in some way that I couldn't understand. Here I'd been given this wonderful channel and then I'd somehow lost it. 'What did I do?' I asked myself again and again. 'Where did I go wrong?' It was Jim who finally suggested that possibly my spirit guide had left because it was now time for me to assume total responsibility for what I was doing. I meditated on this and, after a time, the Hindu appeared once more. All he said was 'good-bye.' I got the message. I was on my own."

The period that followed was very difficult for Anne. "I felt that good and bad, life and death were fighting a war and I was the battleground," she explains. "I saw all kinds of visions, most of them unpleasant. For weeks it seemed that a skeleton followed me everywhere I went. It really didn't help at all to know that I was the only one who saw it. During that same period I had my chest X-rayed and was told that I had tuberculosis. The news was almost welcome. It offered an opportunity to let go, to postpone my duties until another lifetime."

Anne believes today that she herself created both the skeleton and the TB spot. "Energy exists," she says. "It's real. If you want to die, you will attract a killer of one kind or another. As soon as I made the decision to live, the skeleton and the spot both disappeared. Both originally existed just as energy exists, but it was I who created them and I who took them away. Power, energy—it's all out there waiting to be used for good or for bad. Everything that has existed still exists and can be reconstructed atom for atom. One day I know a camera will be invented that can photograph the past and the future. We can all of us create or destroy by applying tension. The so-called impending catastrophe in California is a wonderful example. If enough people worry about it, expend energy thinking about it, planning for it, etc., it will certainly come about. *But it doesn't have to.*"

Anne's mediumship began to evolve in 1961 when Dr. Irene Hickman placed an unopened medical folder in her hands. "I'm not sure how to proceed with this one. What do you think?" she asked.

Without knowing anything about the patient, Anne was able to tune in on the problem. "Her headaches are caused by a weak muscle in the left eye," she diagnosed. "This condition should be checked immediately and corrected before it grows any worse. Glasses are needed, a small prism. It can be easily attended to, but she should see an oculist right away."

Another time Anne described the symptoms disturbing a patient—unknown to her—as being caused by low stomach acid. "He should take a few drops of diluted hydrochloric acid with his meals," she advised.

"Good, that checks out very well," Dr. Hickman agreed. "I'll prescribe a few drops of diluted hydrochloric acid to be taken with each meal."

"I think plain vinegar would be even better," Anne suggested. "It should be easier on the few teeth he has left."

More dramatic assistance came when Irene presented Anne with the folder of Laura H., a woman suffering from a severe nervous disorder. Unknown to Anne, Laura H. had in the preceding few months become almost a complete recluse. Her once happy, outgoing nature had changed to one of extreme depression and fear of the unknown. Unexplained hysteria had caused Laura to be fired from a responsible position as a legal secretary. She had retreated further and further into a protective shell, rejecting the social advances of a once large circle of friends. During the day she remained at home alone, for she had suddenly developed an intense fear of driving her car. Laura's nights were plagued by insomnia. She had become a virtual prisoner and yet had been unable to explain the nature of her fears to Dr. Hickman.

"The problem is not with the patient; it's with her dead sister," Anne said, looking down at the unopened folder. "This woman passed over a few months ago but refuses to let go of her live sister. No wonder the poor patient feels that someone is watching her all the time.

Someone really is."

Addressing the spirit aloud, Anne said. "You're not helping her; you're not helping at all. Your work on earth is done for now. Perhaps you will have another chance in the next life time—in other circumstances—but not now. Your sister needs to express herself, to grow as an individual. You wouldn't want her to be an emotional cripple when she passes over, would you? Our life on earth is like a school. We're here to grow physically, mentally, and spiritually. Surely you've discovered that by now."

Anne quickly found the spirit to be a determined adversary, an entity very much bound to the earthly world and particularly to the life of her younger sister. "What will happen to Laura if I don't take care of her?" she demanded to know.

"Your presence is hurting Laura. She knows that something is hovering near her, but she doesn't know what it is. She's very frightened. Just back off for a little while and then observe how the fear goes with you," Anne urged.

The spirit appeared to waver, admitting at last, "At night I stand by her bedside and try to cover her. I touch her forehead and she awakens and does seem rather disturbed. But I meant no harm. I only want to help Laura."

Anne promised to explain the spirit's good intentions, but urged again that she absent herself for a time. "Why don't you work with people in your new realm? Talk with them, watch over and encourage them as you try to do with Laura," she suggested.

"But I haven't anyone here."

"They will come," Anne assured her. "Aren't your mother and father with you?"

"No, I haven't even taken time to look for them. I haven't looked for anybody. I wanted to be with Laura."

"Perhaps it's time you did."

"That could be interesting," the spirit considered. "You know I'm really quite bright. I feel though as if my mind had not been used properly and needs stimulation."

"In this life you were limited by a body that was not well. But now you're whole and strong," Anne reminded her.

"Yes, that's true. I can actually think a book here. I don't have to waste time sitting at a typewriter. Why, I can even think beautiful thoughts into Laura's head!"

"Well, yes, I suppose you could, but why don't you concentrate your efforts now on the higher realms. Exercise your mind there and then later on you can think those thoughts to Laura—if you still want to. This is just the beginning of endless wonderful adventures for you," Anne assured her.

"Oh, it's so hard to give up. But I do see, I was very wrong. I loved Laura but I was jealous of her. There were so many things that she could do that I couldn't. She was very pretty and I wanted so much to be like her."

"Do you know why you became ill in this life?"

"I quit growing inside. I shriveled up inwardly and then my physical body became ill. It was just that simple— I shriveled up."

"Now you're at another crossroads where you can choose to grow or to remain shriveled," Anne reminded her. "What will your choice be this time?"

"I want to grow. I want to grow!"

"Then stop hanging around this plane," Anne advised. "Leave Laura and go on to your own development. You're no longer confined. Your body is healthy and free."

"Yes, it's a beautiful color even—almost transparent. I hadn't even looked at myself. I've been so busy with Laura that I never even bothered to notice the changes in myself." The spirit, now thoroughly contrite, admitted that she had been constantly hovering over the unfortunate Laura. "When she drove her car, I was always there saying, 'Do this,' 'Don't do that or you'll have an accident.' No wonder she was afraid. Perhaps I did that in life as well."

"Maybe you did," Anne agreed, "but you don't have to do it now. You have a wonderful new life of your own to lead."

This rather bizarre exchange tape-recorded by Dr. Hickman—with Anne speaking in two voices, her own and another quite different—coincided with the abrupt recovery of Laura H., who suddenly appeared to her startled friends as a new woman.

The patient's insomnia completely disappeared. No longer reluctant to drive her car, she quickly returned to her former gregarious ways. Fortunately Laura's former excellent work record made it easy to find a new job. "I'm happier than I've ever been and have a wonderful sense of freedom that's quite new to me," she told Irene Hickman.

As for the earthbound spirit? Presumably she has moved on to better things. Anne never had occasion to contact her again.

"Most problems are far more prosaic than Laura H.'s," Anne says, "but they can be every bit as troublesome. Often the afflicted individual—like Laura—doesn't know herself what the trouble is. My psychic ability enables me to tune in and put a handle on it."

In this manner Anne functions as a kind of "family therapist," bridging the gap between the physical and spiritual realms in order to alleviate many different kinds of problems. Once a middle-aged woman came to Anne for comfort. Her teen-age daughter had died only a few days before in an automobile accident. Theirs had been a stormy relationship, for the daughter, a sensitive, questing young woman, seemed to be dominated by a self-destructive passion that frequently brought her into open conflict with her mother. Only an hour before the accident the two had had an angry quarrel, which erupted when the girl had insisted upon going out with a very reckless young man. Now the mother was consumed with guilt. Could she have prevented the tragedy? Might she even have been its indirect cause? These relentless self-accusations coupled with the loss of her beloved child had caused great torment.

Anne listened quietly to the story and then mentally detached herself, slipping into a deep trance. Her lips moved but the voice was no longer that of Anne Armstrong. Its tone and pitch were completely different.

"You're my daughter! That's her voice; I'd know it anywhere!" the bewildered woman exclaimed.

"Don't worry about me, mother. I'm happy here, studying and continuing to write my poetry."

"My daughter is an excellent poet," the mother interrupted excitedly.

Anne continued, unaware of her reaction. "You didn't cause my death. I really wanted to die. I wasn't ready for that life. Reality was too harsh for me to deal with. I wanted out. I wanted to come home—to this home. I'm resting now, studying and writing. I'll come back to earth and try again when I'm strong enough, but this is right for me now. I'm happy now, so you must be happy for me."

The mother left Anne's home much happier than she had been upon arrival. She was calmer, more reconciled to her loss—which no longer seemed so final. Most important, the crushing guilt was gone.

Anne's work is not by any means confined to the spirit world. Quite often she is able to tune in to special qualities or talents of which the troubled individual is unaware. An example is the well-known raconteur Neil Whitman, who came to Anne for advice when he was a disgruntled schoolteacher, thwarted by bureaucracy and the restrictions of classroom routine. "You're more than a teacher, you're a storyteller. That's what you should be doing," Anne informed him.

Whitman was astounded. "How did you know I love to tell stories?" He confided that he was a kind of "closet" storyteller who delighted in collecting fanciful tales from his travels in the Near East and from obscure books of fables and fairy tales. Relating these to others was his greatest joy. Why not make a career of it? he mused.

Today Whitman has carved an entirely new niche for himself as a professional storyteller and also works as a consultant to schools in the fields of creative writing, drama, dance, and self awareness.

Another troubled individual who found new direction as a result of Anne's psychic insights was Roberta DeLong Miller, a young woman whose life seemed to have reached a standstill. "You could be a healer," Anne told her. "You could do it all with your hands. Tune in to the powers within yourself. They will open up a whole new way of life for you."

The advice—though totally unexpected—seemed right. Roberta DeLong Miller has since brought comfort to thousands. She travels throughout the world lecturing on her unusual healing technique and has recently written a successful book, *Psychic Massage*, in which she describes her methods, evolved from massage yet much more than mere hand manipulations. The addition of psychic awareness makes it possible to heal or balance an individual's mind and emotions through his body.

Psychic Massage bears the dedication, "To Anne Armstrong, who taught me that the body is a tool for spirit."

As Anne's reputation as a medium grew, she was asked to lecture at the University of California at Davis and to present workshops at the Esalen Institute at Big Sur, California. While presenting a seminar at Davis, Anne made the acquaintance of Dr. Harold Puthoff, a scientist employed by the Stanford Research Institute in Menlo Park, California.

Dr. Puthoff was so impressed by her uncanny ability that he came to Anne himself for a psychic reading. Her predictions seemed unlikely at the time but "all came true," he reported later.

Later when Puthoff and his SRI associate, Dr. Russell Targ, undertook a research project sponsored by the Foundation for Parasensory Investigation in New York City and the Institute of Noetic Sciences in Palo Alto, California, they sought Anne's participation as a consultant. As a result of more than a year and a half of intensive study and exhaustive laboratory experiments, the two scientists published evidence, indicating that many persons have the ability to send and receive information through a strange and as yet unexplained power. Writing in the October 1974 issue of *Nature*, a prestigious British scientific journal, they concluded that this ability was not extrasensory perception, but something "that depended on an unknown seldom exercised sensory capability."

Dr. Targ stated that Anne's contribution was invaluable to the project, which involved, among other psychics, the famous "spoon bender," Uri Geller, and Pat Price, a former California police commissioner able to receive telepathic communication.

"My part was really easy," Anne says. "Being psychic myself, I could readily understand the mechanics of what was going on in a way that the scientists could not. As an objective party I was often able to suggest new techniques that had not occurred to the psychic under investigation because he was too close to the problem. It wasn't even necessary for me to meet the psychic involved in order to tune in to the specific difficulty—after all, that's what being a psychic really means. Quite a number of times Doctors Puthoff and Targ simply came to the house and tape-recorded my suggestions for use in the laboratory."

Anne has been presenting workshops at the Esalen Institute since 1967 and has worked with a variety of psychiatrists there and elsewhere. "It really doesn't matter to them whether I lived a life as Antonius or not," she explains. "Some accept the validity of reincarnation while others prefer to equate the whole thing in terms of Jungian symbolism. The important thing is that I am able to use my psychic ability frequently to facilitate psychotherapy. Psychoanalysis is a trial-and-error procedure. The psychiatrist must first find out what's wrong before he or she can attempt to clear it up. This is very difficult when the patient doesn't know himself—which is often the case. I can tune in, find the hidden cause triggering the illness; and then doctor and patient can go to work together on a cure."

After Anne's spirit guide had departed, leaving her on her own, at first she felt it best to give readings with her eyes closed. "I was afraid that I might be influenced by the reactions of the person I was working with," she explained. "I didn't want any of the material coming through to be contaminated. This is no longer necessary. I know what I know; it's all right there before me."

Problems concerning children often come up at workshops, and quite frequently Anne is able to give a very special kind of insight. Two such cases occurred during the spring of 1975.

"One woman was particularly distraught as she related the serious difficulties that she was having with her teenage daughter," Anne recalls. " 'There really isn't anything that you can do right now,' I explained to her. 'Within a week your daughter will run away. No harm will come to her and eventually she will return to you.' Well, of course she wasn't too happy to hear that her daughter was going to run away. But in another sense this was rather comforting news. The woman had the option—which she took—of trying very hard to ease the situation with her daughter. When she pursued every avenue within her power and the girl still left home, she at least had the satisfaction of knowing that she had fought the good fight. Imagine how much worse it would have been for her without the warning? Suppose the week had simply moved along in the customary unhappy pattern with possibly an angry quarrel preceding the girl's leaving. In place of anxiety and guilt, this woman had confidence in the future. She was able to detach herself from her daughter's identity crisis and concentrate on improving her own life."

Another mother discussed her frustration with a young son who was doing very poorly in elementary school. Though the boy was intelligent, he seemed to have great difficulties in any situation involving time. Even putting on his coat and boots prior to school recess was a highly traumatic experience. If there was any element of pressure involved, he was totally unable to coordinate his efforts. The hostility, impatience, and sense of failure resulting from this problem were seriously affecting both the boy's schoolwork and his social life. The friction at home is easy to imagine.

"As I listened to that weary young mother catalog a series of problems that had arisen, I suddenly knew exactly what was to blame," Anne recalls. 'Something went wrong when your boy was born, didn't it?' I said.

" 'Did it ever!' she replied. 'He was supposed to be born at home. A neighbor—a man who claimed to know all about midwifery—was to deliver him. I was very happy at the idea of my baby being born among pleasant surroundings, very confident of the results. When I went into labor I was full of pleasant expectations. But then my neighbor completely panicked. When he saw that the baby was about to arrive, he insisted that I would have to go to the hospital. The baby's birth was forcibly delayed while I was driven forty miles over a rough, winding mountain road.'

" 'There's your problem,' I pointed out. 'Your boy entered this life confused and is still confused. Any problem connected with time touches off a submerged memory of this early trauma— his introduction to life.'

"Since this was a very modern young woman who believed in absolute frankness with her boy, there were no problems connected with explaining to the child exactly what had happened. 'None of it was your fault,' she reminded him. 'You were ready to go; it was the rest of us who goofed. No one's holding you back now. You're on your own time, moving in your own way, at your own speed. Relax and enjoy it.'

"I'm happy to say the child responded beautifully. He understood his mother's message perfectly and now functions with dexterity equal to any of his classmates. He's very happy and so are those close to him."

Anne works most frequently with Mary Jane Ledyard, a Woodside, California psychiatrist who first heard her lecture and then went for a reading. "We were instant friends," Dr. Ledyard recalls, "as though we had known, liked, and trusted one another before. A working relationship developed from our close friendship. Anne's special ability supplements my training as a psychotherapist perfectly. Our skills are very different but they mesh so completely that it's hard to tell where one leaves off and the other begins. Anne has the remarkable ability to look right inside the individual and know exactly where they are in terms of their own development. This is tremendously helpful when choicemaking situations are involved. She's very good on broad, long range goals—defining them and facilitating progression—and that's what life's all about, isn't it? I really don't know anyone more adept at bringing out the very best potentials—no matter how deeply they appear to be hidden."

Anne's own life has evolved in a manner that would have seemed incredible to the repressed housewife who first consulted Irene Hickman in October 1959. She no longer lives with her engineer husband, preferring to retain her own lifestyle.

"I suppose you might call it an open marriage," she explains. "After more than thirty-five years and who knows how many lifetimes, it seems very right that I be on my own. Jim lives in a different city now, working at his career as I continue to work at mine. We both need to be in an environment where we can grow as individuals. At this point, it doesn't happen to be the same environment. He understands this very well; we're close friends. Why wouldn't we be—think of all we've been through together!"

Thelma Moss

Past Mistress at ESPionage

"What kind of fool am I?" is a question that Thelma Moss may ask herself upon occasion. But far more frequently it is her disapproving colleagues who ask the question for her.

Dr. Thelma Moss, a medical psychologist and associate professor at the Neuropsychiatric Institute at UCLA, is considered the arch kook of academia. More accurately, she is a kind of modern-day frontier scout. Her territory is the untracked realm of the human mind. Instead of arrows or tomahawks, she dodges the verbal attacks of her associates. Though Dr. Moss' psychic research has earned her worldwide renown, she works under the constant threat of dismissal. She has presented critically acclaimed papers at international conferences in Moscow and Prague, but at home finds it necessary to fund her own research.

"At the present time the university neither encourages nor discourages me," she explains. "They merely provide a small room. What I do there is up to me. Many of my associates warn that I'm committing professional suicide to do anything."

Currently this 20-by-20-foot "lab" contains a small desk, an equally small table, three uncomfortable chairs, and an ancient filing cabinet. The rest of the space is taken up by a large structure that looks very like a meat-storage locker. Next to its heavy metal latch is the reassuring sign, "You cannot be locked in." Behind the heavy doors of the locker, a variety of dramatic experiments have taken place. It has been used as an isolation booth for telepathy testing, as a darkroom for developing Kirlian photography, as a seance room for experiments to investigate mediumship, and even as a mini-medical center for faith-healing attempts.

All kinds of people take part in the experiments. "The staff is purely voluntary and includes everyone from doctors to stage hypnotists," she says. "No one is paid. I buy all the equipment myself. All of us involved in this parapsychology thing are terribly broke. Sometimes I wonder if the 'put up or shut up' attitude necessary to do this kind of work isn't a part of a master plan. Whether we like it or not, psychic researchers do seem to demonstrate a negation of materialism."

As unconcerned with official status as she is with monetary rewards, Thelma appears ready to take on anything and everything. It's generally accepted that college professors simply do not chase ghosts. But that hasn't stopped Thelma from investigating numerous haunted houses.

"Of course this opens up the whole idea of survival phenomena which people generally prefer to ignore. Death is an unpopular subject for most—and why wouldn't it be? Tradition tells us that the vast majority of the world's population are doomed to hell for all eternity. The alternative—playing a harp forever—sounds pretty damn dull. So

Thelma Moss

John Larsen, Psychic Magazine

many prefer to write the whole thing off as a bad joke. 'Eat, drink, and be merry,' they advise, 'because there is nothing out there.'

"I believe that fear stands in the way of most survival research. The majority of scientists prefer not to challenge a comfortable belief structure. They've come to terms with a wholly materialistic viewpoint; they're at ease with it and don't enjoy being challenged. Fortunately or otherwise, there are a foolhardy few of us who say, 'Let's look, let's question, whatever happens, we'll critically examine it.'"

Thelma's own path to personal discovery and awareness has been circuitous. As a child growing up in Bridgeport, Connecticut, she had no thought of being anything other than an actress. Both her father, A. C. Schnee, who operated a real estate business, and her mother were nonreligious. Thelma, her older brother, and younger sister were raised in a casual, nonquestioning atmosphere. "We were all very much occupied with the here and the now, with not much thought given to anything else," she recalls.

After completing a year at Wellesley College near Boston, she transferred to the drama department of Carnegie Institute of Technology in Pittsburgh. Upon receiving her bachelor's degree in drama in 1939, Thelma headed straight for New York City and a successful stage career that would be the focal point of her life for the next twenty years. During this time she met and married Paul Moss, a theatrical and film producer, and had two children. During their married years the Mosses worked together presenting plays and films written or acted in by Mrs. Moss. These were busy, exciting years during which Thelma appeared with Ethel Barrymore in *The Corn Is Green* and with Alfred Lunt and Lynn Fontanne in *The Sea Gull*. She wrote numerous stage, movie, and television plays, including the screenplay *The Detective*, starring Alec Guiness, and *Father Brown* with Guiness and Peter Finch.

Despite her many critically acclaimed successes, the world of the theater lost much of its allure for Thelma when her husband died suddenly of a heart attack. This great personal loss was the cause of much sadness and finally led her to seek professional therapeutic help. An offshoot of psychotherapy was the daring decision to try LSD.

"Why did I submit to the experiment?" she asked in her account of the experience, *My Self and I*, a book, now out of print, written under the pseudonymn Constance Newland. "I did not know the answer to that question then. It was only after my explorations were done that I found an answer: I had been propelled by a strong unconscious motive. That answer would never have satisfied me when I originally volunteered for the experiment because, at the time, I did not accept the unconscious mind except as an interesting abstraction of small pragmatic value.

"During the course of therapy I traveled deep into those remarkable regions of the mind and came upon a series of illuminations. I found that in addition to being *consciously* a loving mother and respectable citizen I was also, *unconsciously*, a murderess, a pervert, a cannibal, a sadist and a masochist. In the wake of these dreadful discoveries, I lost my fear of dentists, the clicking in my neck and throat, the arm tensions and my dislike of a clock ticking in my bedroom. I also achieved transcendent sexual fulfillment."

One of the most dramatic occurrences that happened as a spin-off of the LSD experience took place early one morning when Thelma awakened from a sound sleep with the strong impulse to write. Ignoring the clock which read 5 A.M., she reached for a pencil and pad and obediently began.

"As I watched my fingers literally fly across the paper, I realized that what I was doing was a form of automatic writing," she recalls today. "The words were just coming through the pencil and being put down on paper without any conscious awareness on my part of the subject matter. After that first experience, for about four months I would get the same kind of impulse to write late at night or very early in the morning. Usually what came out was poetry—

pretty good poetry, it seemed to me. And the strangest thing is that I've never written poetry before that four-month period—or since. The only way you can describe the experience—or the poetry—was mystical. Here's an example:

'There is nothing in the world
More marvelous than I
The living, breathing miracle of I.
The I of him, the I of thee
And, too, the I of me.'

"That 'I'—the godhead—exists for everybody and that sudden knowledge of it, along with the other manifestations of transcendental awareness that were revealing themselves through LSD, compelled me to return to college. I was determined to learn everything possible about psychology, physiology, learning theory, and theories of personality. The more I studied, the more fascinated I became with the whole frontier of scientific exploration: the interrelation of body and mind. Suddenly almost without realizing it, I had become a middle-aged college girl intent on a new career in psychic research."

Thelma Moss abandoned her successful dramatic career and returned to school in 1959. By 1960, she had obtained her bachelor's degree in psychology from UCLA and entered the UCLA graduate school of psychology to work toward her doctorate—training at Wadsworth Hospital, Veterans Administration Center in Los Angeles, and at Mt. Sinai Hospital, also in Los Angeles, and at UCLA's Neuropsychiatric Institute.

She received her doctorate in psychology from UCLA in 1966, becoming at that time both a medical psychologist and an assistant professor at the institute, positions that she holds today. Vestiges of Thelma Moss the actress survive in the husky, well-modulated voice, a manner of speaking that reminds one a little of Susan Hayward. Dr. Moss's wide range of expression, her dramatic delivery of even more dramatic material makes for a compelling presentation on the lecture platform.

In evaluating the experience with psychedelics after more than fifteen years, Thelma feels that she has received immense benefits from LSD therapy but has no desire to continue with this type of experimentation. "After a while it can become a crutch," she explains. "Now that I've learned the technique of transcendental meditation, I'd rather do it myself. The psychedelics pose such a dilemna. They can at times be devastating, demoralizing—even psychosis producing. I know this very well, having experienced some real bummers myself. But, at the other extreme, they can be a highly transcendental experience and often productive of psychic phenomena. Unfortunately no one can predict or control the direction of the trip. That's why these drugs should be approached with extreme caution and deep respect. Certainly no one should attempt this kind of experience without very good supervision, and I don't mean Tim Leary's type of supervision either.

"I think LSD lets down our defenses so that all kinds of unconscious forces erupt into awareness. Sometimes the power is so great that some of us are overwhelmed—and remain overwhelmed long after the drugs have disappeared from the body. It's certainly essential that people trained in understanding the nature of the unconscious and symbolic processes be present, people who can recognize a warning signal and react quickly. Believe me, mad trips can be pretty awful even under proper medical supervision. It could be a terrifying and possibly dangerous experience to be alone with no place to turn to for help. Only a fool would take such a chance. Perhaps that's why so many have left drugs and gone into the meditative disciplines such as transcendental meditation. Meditation enables us to explore the fascinating dimensions of the mind more gradually and with more control and safety than LSD."

Thelma Moss believes that the drug culture that was so much a part of the sixties scene is largely responsible for the interest in parapsychology today. "As the young people began to experiment with psychedelic drugs, they learned either firsthand or from friends' accounts about isolated, brief incidences of clairvoyance, out of the body travel, telepathy, expanded awareness and past life remembrances—occurrences far beyond the normal range of experience," she explains.

"Though much of this has not been investigated and may be delusional, there is documented evidence of psychic phenomena occurring during therapeutic experiences that's very convincing. The reaction to all this has often been a withdrawal from materialistic values and conventional standards of behavior. Change is in the air, and perhaps it is this that the Establishment—universities and other large institutions—fears most. Change can be very threatening; emotional retooling very costly."

Another factor instrumental in advancing the progress of psychic investigation comes from an unexpected quarter: electronics. "Scientists working in the field of electronics and some physicists have become fascinated by the awareness that their own chemistry can affect machinery," she says.

"It's a kind of brown-thumb thing. Now that there are machines that can measure the effect that two different individuals may have on the same machine at the same time, the phenomenon ceases to be metaphysical. It's a known factor, demanding scientific investigation and study. The same people who work with computers and transistors have found that they can get some very strange phenomena when working with certain kinds of advanced equipment. Now some of them are open to the idea that maybe we can one day dispense with our elaborate instrumentation and communicate without it. Is that really so far out? Russian scientists don't seem to think so. They are conducting telepathy experiments right now—government-funded experiments—in an effort to communicate with their cosmonauts.

"In our own country two specialists in electronics

communication using the electromyograph discovered the very same frequencies which are used to transmit transatlantic radio messages *in the human muscle*. It may be that the human body has transmitters and receivers that are too delicate to be detected with the primitive equipment that we are using today. But tomorrow? Who knows?"

Thelma obviously isn't waiting until tomorrow to conduct her own experiments in the field of telepathy. While only a graduate student, she noted in studying the literature of telepathic phenomena that the majority of instances occurred when the transmitter was under emotional stress. Pioneer experiments conducted by Dr. J. B. Rhine at Duke University utilized cards inscribed with one of four simple symbols. The transmitter would attempt to convey an impression of the symbol on which he was focusing his attention to a receiver in an adjoining room. The results of the experiment were encouraging, but Thelma felt they would be even more conclusive if the significant emotional factor could be added to the experiment.

The idea of emotional ESP sounded "crazy" to her associates, but she persisted. In an effort to duplicate to whatever degree possible in a laboratory setting the strong effects that generally accompany telepathic events, an entirely new extrasensory perception experiment was created by the innovative and tenacious psychic investigator. It began with the selection of volunteer subjects, who ranged in age from sixteen to sixty-five and in occupation from high school students and housewives to airline pilots and doctors. All believed that they had some form of psychic ability, and four were professional mediums. "By selecting individuals with such diverse backgrounds I hoped to keep any possible leakage of information concerning the proposed stimuli at a minimum," she explained.

"Thirty pairs of transmitters and receivers were selected. Each team of receiver and transmitter were well known to one another on the assumption that telepathy occurs most frequently in people with strong rapport. Other volunteer subjects worked as receivers only; but in this aspect of the experiment the stimuli was shown to a mannequin that had been placed in the isolation booth rather than to a human being. There was no transmitter."

The experiment began with the physical separation of the transmitter and the receiver. The transmitter was sent into the lab's isolation booth where she or he was bombarded visually and aurally by emotionally charged stimuli. After each stimulus episode, the transmitter was asked to describe his reactions in detail. This was recorded verbatim on the spot.

At the same time the receiver was taken to a dimly lit room (about seventy-five feet down the hall) and asked to report his or her stream of consciousness, which was also recorded in its entirety. In this manner it was hoped that strong emotional episodes were being experienced and expressed by the transmitter and then "sent" to the receiver.

Throughout the session the transmitter was closeted in the soundproof isolation booth. Distraction in the darkened chamber was minimal, rendering the transmitter a captive audience literally forced to focus on the stimuli, which took the form of 35mm color or black-and-white slides flashed by Kodak carousel projector onto a screen placed directly over the glass aperture of the booth.

As an accompaniment to the slides, musical selections were played on a tape recorder directly into the earphones worn by the transmitter. An experimenter, also wearing earphones, who was stationed just outside the isolation booth, monitored the music.

Another tape recorder was utilized, one channel recording the transmitter's reactions at the end of each episode of stimulation and the other channel recording the receiver's impressions in the next room via a microphone.

In the other room designated for the experiment, the receiver relaxed on a couch. A second experimenter remained in the room behind a folding screen. Beside her on a table, also behind the screen, was a light box which signaled when it was time to pull aside the screen and ask the receiver to communicate his or her impressions. Once the experiment was in progress, the light box was the only means of communication between the two experimenters.

Describing the procedure in an article, "Telepathy and Emotional Stimuli," which appeared in a 1967 issue of the *Journal of Abnormal Psychology*—one of a scant handful published on parapsychology in the journal's seventy-five-year history—Thelma Moss explained that the episodes were numbered from one to six. Their sequence was determined spontaneously by each individual transmitter, who would be asked at the beginning of the session to choose a number between one and six. If three was selected, the transmitter would be shown episode three. After the transmitter's reactions were recorded, another selection would be made with number three omitted. This procedure continued until all six of the episodes had been experienced.

"In other words, the transmitter selected his or her own sequence of episodes *unknown to anyone*," Dr. Moss emphasized. "This was considered an important control, since presumably neither the transmitter nor the receiver knew what the numbers represented."

The objective descriptions numbered below were used verbatim as the episode cards in the judging procedure:

1. *President Kennedy's Assassination.* This started with JFK's voice delivering part of his inaugural address, which ended with, "Ask not what your country can do for you; ask rather what you can do for your country." With these words a picture of the President was flashed on the screen. Next came the song *In the Summer of His Years*, describing the day of the murder.

Accompanying the music was a series of slides: the

smiling President and his wife carrying a bouquet of roses arriving at the Dallas Airport; two slides of the automobile stopped on the street, Jackie climbing on the back for help; Robert Kennedy and Jackie, still in her blood-stained suit, leaving Dallas at night; the flag-draped bier at night illuminated with the White House in the background. Once more President Kennedy's voice saying, "Ask not what your country can do for you; ask rather what you can do for your country."

(Expected reactions were sharp grief, sorrow, horror, etc.)

2. *Ocean.* Several slides in color showing views of the ocean from dawn until sunset. Surf pounding on rocks; the deep blue ocean, resorts at noonday; beaches on the Hawaiian Islands with bathers and sailboats on the water; and a view of a mountain lake at sunset framed by pine trees rising from the cliffs of the mountain. Throughout the presentation a tape of Respighi's *Fountains of Rome* was played.

(Expected reactions were relaxation, serenity, peace, etc.)

3. *Nazis.* Throughout the episode, one short passage from Mossolov's *Iron Foundry* was repeated over and over; piercing, discordant—and played at a volume meant to be uncomfortable and irritating. It accompanied an assortment of slides: a Nazi rally showing huge red banners emblazoned with swastikas; the devastation inside a concentration camp; a close view of the cremating ovens; a wagon filled with rotting corpses. Views of the skeleton-like survivors.

(Expected reactions were shock, disgust, hatred, fury, etc.)

4. *Ladies.* The tape played throughout featured jazz music, David Rose's *The Stripper* with its exaggerated

drumbeat. Several slides were shown of draped and un-draped girls of the *Playboy* genre: blondes, brunettes, redheads. All in color. Primarily beautiful, sensuous bodies.

(Expected reactions were excitement, arousal, desire, etc.)

5. *Cold.* Each transmitter was asked to keep his or her left foot in a bucket of ice and water for at least forty seconds.

(Expected reactions were cold, numbness, tingling, pain, etc.)

6. *Disneyland.* To the accompaniment of *Tuxedo Junction*, colored slides of Disneyland were shown: the freeways, Mickey Mouse entrance, trolleys, cable cars, the Matterhorn, the Mad Tea Party ride, etc., always featuring crowds of people and a festive atmosphere.

(Expected reactions were amusement, gaiety, fun, etc.)

Meanwhile, just down the hall, the receiver had been given the following instructions:

"Please make yourself comfortable. We're going to leave you now, so relax and hopefully feel free enough to be receptive to what's happening in the other room. At certain times, I'll push aside the screen and ask you to report whatever impressions, sensations, images or feelings you've had during that period. Please report everything that may have come to mind no matter how strange or foolish it might seem. You may have a lot to report, but if you've had no impressions at all, simply say so. Whatever you say will be recorded from the microphone around your neck into the stereo recorder that you saw in the other room."

When the second experimenter received indication via the light box that the first episode was positioned and ready to go, she pushed aside the screen and announced to the receiver who was resting on the couch that the experiment was about to begin.

"Just relax and receive," she suggested, then closed the screen and signaled a return flash to her co-worker waiting outside the isolation booth to indicate that the receiver was ready.

The episode was presented to the transmitter and at its conclusion he or she was told to report any reactions. *At the same time* the first experimenter signaled three light flashes to her co-worker, who then asked the receiver to describe her or his impressions during the previous interval. In this way both the reactions of the transmitter and the impressions of the receiver were recorded on two different channels at approximately the same time.

An interval of neutral music was played to the transmitter in the isolation booth and then the procedure was repeated with a new set of stimuli.

With the subjects forming the control group—each delegated a receiver—the same process was followed except that the mannequin replaced the transmitter in the isolation booth. Receivers were not told of this substitution. Rather, it was explained that for experimental reasons the transmitter was to remain a stranger.

After all the sessions had been completed, the tapes were transcribed verbatim on identical typewritten cards, a separate card being used for each episode of each transmitter's reactions and each receiver's impressions. The results were then matched by twelve professional psychologists and psychiatrists, who found strong evidence for telepathy. A dramatic example is that none of the receivers in the control group ("working" with the mannequin) picked up on the "cold" episode, while 55 per cent of the regular receivers did.

Descriptions of seascapes, water, etc., were reported

by 80 per cent of the receivers working with transmitters but only by 33 per cent of those without. In the latter case, some possibility of telepathy still existed, for the experimenter was both watching and listening to the stimuli being presented to the mannequin.

There were some dramatic incidences of direct hits by receivers coinciding exactly with the reactions of their transmitter in the isolation booth. An example was the "ocean" sequence in which the impressions of the receiver were specificically described as Hawaiian. "I seem to be in Honolulu," the receiving subject said. "I see palm trees, bright colored flowers, people swimming. There's a holiday atmosphere, a sense of rest and relaxation."

The assassination episode also triggered vivid impressions. "I have a feeling of sadness," one receiver said. "It's as if I were crying, or something tragic has happened and I'm grieving over something much the same as one might feel attending a funeral of a dear friend or possibly a well-known public figure in whom one had faith."

It is interesting that the only proper name mentioned more than once in the study was that of President Kennedy, who was named by five different receivers working with live transmitters but by none of the control group.

Oftentimes the hits scored were symbolic rather than literal descriptions of the episode actually observed by the transmitter. A male receiver envisioned a lot of bunnies scampering around a field during the *Playboy* episode. Another was reminded of the popular discothèque, "Whiskey à Go Go," on Sunset Strip.

A different receiver during the Disneyland sequence said, "I see lots of balloons," (there were none among the slides, though they are certainly a common sight at Disneyland) and "I feel myself whirling around in a teacup."

Another described—without actually naming—Disneyland most accurately: "The Swiss Alps, the Matterhorn, ice cream cones, little boys, little cable cars."

One of the most intriguing factors were the many

occurrences of dramatic mismatching. For instance, while the transmitter was describing the ocean episode, the receiver got strong impressions of President Kennedy and the specific song, *In The Summer of His Years*. Then a few moments later, as the transmitter was describing the Kennedy assassination episode, the receiver began to feel an intense coldness. The next episode to be experienced by the transmitter was the cold sequence. One possible explanation for this phenomena could be precognition.

Dr. Moss went on to repeat the experiment numerous times, with results that she describes as "statistically significant"—often with odds better than 1000 to 1. Surprisingly, in a long-distance experiment arranged with parapsychologists in New York and Sussex, England, the results proved just as impressive as when the receivers were only seventy-five feet down the hall.

Writing four years later, once more in the *Journal of Abnormal Psychology*, Thelma further clarified the rationale behind the emotional ESP experiment. "The ultimate objective in these studies is to learn, if possible, by what psychological process telepathy occurs. If this can be done, we may begin to refine what is obviously at present very crude transmission (much noise, little signal) in order to produce consistent, recognizable demonstrations of telepathic transmission in the laboratory."

Privately she postulates that telepathy may one day substitute for radio, television, or telephone as a means of communication. "Isn't it odd," she asks, "that science-fiction writers predicted that man would walk on the moon and that we would live to see it, but they never predicted that we would see it on television in our own living rooms! I don't think it's such a big step from looking at men on the moon on your television screen to looking at men on the moon in your head—and really seeing them. Who knows, maybe one day we'll even invent a camera that photographs the past or future. I think a few scientists are hovering on the fringes of the time thing right now.

Perhaps whoever unlocks that barrier will also unlock the riddle of ESP."

Though Thelma Moss has not yet invented a camera that photographs the past or future, she is currently pioneering the use of a camera—or noncamera—almost as revolutionary. It is a device that appears to photograph the life force of individuals and plants.

The technique is called Kirlian photography, after the Russian couple Semyon and Valentina Kirlian, who invented or rediscovered it. The process involves a means of taking pictures, without benefit of a camera or lens, simply by passing a spark of electricity through an object—animal, vegetable, or mineral— while it is in contact with the film.

Definitions of what is photographed vary. Some call it "energy fields," others "bioplasma," "ultrasonic radiation," "bioillumination," "electron emission," or "corona discharge." A far less scientific sounding definition is *"aura"* —a not uncommon phenomenon that psychics have been describing for centuries.

Whatever it is that's being photographed, the resulting picture reveals brilliant patterns within the object and emanations extending beyond it—neither visible to the naked eye. Whatever these emanations may prove to be, it has become clear that they change dramatically within the living organism under special observable conditions.

Dr. Moss first heard of the Kirlian experiments in 1970 and, excited by the possibilities and eager to see firsthand what was happening, went almost immediately to Russia. Returning a few weeks later with an impressive array of Kirlian slides and Russian scientific literature translated specially for her, Thelma's enthusiasm was dampened somewhat by the skepticism of her colleagues, who dismissed the whole technique as "nonsense" and the slides as "contrived fakes." The reactions of electronics engineers were even more dismaying. Most felt that the Kirlian machine—if it could be built at all—would be highly dangerous to experimenter and subject alike.

"Finally I simply stopped talking about the Kirlian concept to associates; they just were not interested," Thelma recalls today. "It was discouraging, but that didn't stop me from thinking about it and speculating about the implications. Then a few months later while teaching the course, Psyche and Psychic Phenomena at UCLA, I devoted a whole evening's lecture time to what I had learned of the Russian research. Afterwards a student came up and said that he'd like to try Kirlian photography. I'll have to admit that I was almost as discouraging as my associates had been to me, but fortunately I did loan him some of my literature.

"A few weeks later the same young man, Kendall Johnson, handed me a photograph of a leaf. It looked astonishingly like a Kirlian specimen. 'Where did you get this?' I gasped.

"He grinned, obviously very pleased with himself. 'In my father-in-law's garage.' It later developed that Ken had studied the literature carefully, particularly the pictures, and then made the rounds of various junk shops until he found everything that resembled the illustrations that I'd given him. Using a collection of flashlight batteries, automobile spark coils, and even an old doorbell, this young insurance claims adjuster had become the first American to master Kirlian photography."

Working together, Thelma and her student have completed a series of innovative experiments that have opened up an entire new realm of conjecture regarding the human consciousness.

One of the most dramatic of the early experiments was the photographing of a "common" leaf, which revealed a complex luminescent pattern of myriad dots and rays that cannot otherwise be seen. Next a portion of the leaf (plucked from a *Plectanthus Australia*, or "Creeping Charlie" plant) was slashed away and the remainder photographed again. A phantom outline of the original leaf remained for several hours and then slowly faded away.

This phenomenon bears a striking resemblance to the phantom limb pain that torments recent amputees, who complain of intense pain in the area where their severed limb *had been*.

The special conditions under which the life field, or aura seems to change in human beings have also been the subject of a number of experiments at the Moss laboratory. In one, two subjects were instructed to imagine strong physical attraction for one another. When photographed, their finger pads revealed rays of luminescence flashing out, each toward the other. The same couple was then asked to visualize strong dislike or repulsion for each other. The results were equally dramatic. The luminescent rays had retracted completely and there was in fact a dark barrier between the two finger pads.

The ancient Chinese medical procedure of acupuncture was investigated next. According to the acupuncture theory, energy is supposed to flow through the body, entering and exiting at specific points along the meridians or channels. In a healthy individual, this energy remains unimpeded. But should the energy become blocked or possibly released too freely, a balance must be reestablished through the insertion of needles at the acupuncture points.

For at least 5000 years the existence of these meridians and acupuncture points has been accepted without question in the East. Now Kirlian photography has revealed luminescent pulsating points on the skin that actually correspond to the traditional acupuncture points.

The *quieting* effects of meditation upon an individual have been observed by photographing the finger pads of a subject before and after meditation, as have the *stimulating* effects of alcohol before and after drinking. A medical student enthusiastically volunteered for the latter experiment. Upon arrival at the lab—completely sober—his finger pads were photographed. This first picture shows almost no corona, merely a vague semicircle of dots. The second photograph taken after nine ounces of bourbon shows a distinct circle with a rosy glow apparent. By the time the subject had finished his seventeenth drink, he was quite literally "all lit up."

One of Thelma's most far-reaching experiments involved her work with Olga Worrall, possibly the most credible faith healer in the United States. Even the most conventional, science-oriented minds find it difficult to scoff at Olga's amazing record of success. The gifted woman has been healing the sick since 1915 when she was only eight years old and since 1950 has been associate director of the New Life Clinic of the Mount Washington Methodist Church in Baltimore, Maryland.

As a healer, she has discovered that not only humans but also dogs, cats, horses, and even chickens respond to the mystical force. A knowledgable woman with a quick, witty sense of humor, Olga is surprisingly relaxed and unassuming about her gift. "It's a natural talent," she insists, "that everyone possesses to some degree. I am just the channel. The real healing is between the patient and God. A healer is merely one who provides the conditions that permit healing to take place. Doctors experience unconventional healing all the time. They call it spontaneous remission—the disease seemingly cures itself. The reason cannot be explained by them. How do *I* explain it? There's only one explanation. It's God's work. His healing did not end with Jesus. Every good doctor is a born healer. He or she has a calling just as I do.

"There have been many through the ages who have been chosen as channels. I'm very human—just like anyone else. I go to the dentist and the eye doctor, but for some reason I have been chosen to help others. It has been my life."

Though Olga has never received any medical training, she frequently has patients referred to her by doctors who are unable to heal them. One such experience occurred in 1959 when Dr. Howard T. Craven of Baltimore referred to

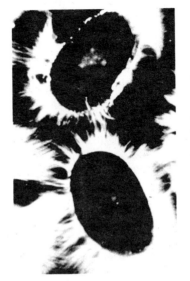

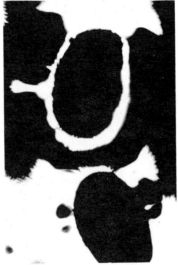

The aura of finger pads of subjects feeling strong attraction

The aura of finger pads of subjects feeling repulsion

The aura shows the whole leaf even after it has been cut

Neuropsychiatric Institute, University of California at Los Angeles

Olga a young nurse who had a large tumor in her abdomen. The woman was in a great deal of pain, had lost thirty-four pounds, and was existing on Demerol.

When Olga laid her hands upon the woman's abdomen, the nurse said that it felt as if a "corkscrew were turning" within her stomach. From that moment on she experienced no more pain, but when she left Olga's clinic the tumor had not been reduced in size. A week later the nurse reported a change. From then on, the tumor continued to diminish until it disappeared entirely. X-rays disclosed no remaining evidence of pathology.

Throughout her long years of healing, Olga Worrall has never received payments, love offerings, thank offerings, etc. Her amazing talents are a gift to all who ask for them.

It is difficult to do follow-up studies because they are so expensive and time consuming. "Sometimes it may be years before I learn the outcome of my work," she admitted once at a lecture sponsored by the Academy of Parapsychology and Medicine at Stanford University. "It's very common to get letters from people who say, 'Seven years ago you cured my arthritis, now would you do something about my husband's hernia.' This may be our first knowledge that the original person was healed."

As eager as Thelma to plum the secrets of the universe, Olga Worrall is an ideal subject for experimentation. She is hopeful that the nature and range of psychic healing can one day be established so that more people may benefit. Thelma Moss's "green thumb" experiments with ailing leaves and Kirlian photography seemed an ideal place to begin.

It had been determined almost immediately that a leaf possessed a life force or eminence that could be photographed. The phantom leaf phenomenon already photographed had clearly demonstrated the gradual "death" of the departed member and finally the leaf itself. Now came the question, could the leaf be saved?

The tradition of the "green thumb" has always been with us. Why not put it to the test? Thelma considered. Quickly following up on her hunch, she sent out a call for anyone believing he or she possessed the power to make plants flourish. Thirty people volunteered and a controlled experiment developed.

The procedure was to take two leaves plucked from the same plant into the isolation booth—now a darkroom. One was the experimental leaf, the other a control. Both were photographed in the normal state, then gashed and photographed again. Then a volunteer "green thumb" was called in and asked to treat one of the injured leaves by placing her or his hands two inches above the surface until it was felt that the leaf had responded and was recovering. Finally both the "healed" leaf and the control leaf were photographed again. In twenty-three out of thirty experiments, a brilliant increase was clearly visible in the luminescence of the healed leaf. The control leaf showed no improvement.

There seems little doubt that the phenomenon could be anything else but an exchange of energy between person and leaf, a dramatic interaction between living organisms.

Now to this experiment came the "big gun," Olga Worrall, a psychic healer capable of saving human lives with her energy field. Great things were expected and received—but not right away.

"The results of Olga's first leaf experiment came as quite a shock to all of us in the lab," Thelma recalls. "We developed the film expecting the leaf that Olga had 'healed' to literally leap out at us lighting up the darkroom with its luminescence. To our surprise, the complete opposite was true. The image of the leaf that Olga had supposedly healed was barely visible. Could it be that this world-famous healer was actually a brown thumb? The very idea of having to tell her was dreadful, but what else could I do?"

Olga received the news with surprising equanimity. "I probably gave the leaf too much power" she said matter of factly. "Tomorrow I'll be a bit more gentle."

The same experiment was repeated the following day, with a milder flow of energy radiating from Olga. The result was a brilliantly flaring leaf completely "cured." It appeared obvious that the faith healer could indeed channel her energy at will.

The possibility that we might all possess the latent ability to dip into this mysterious power source is the driving force behind Thelma Moss' controversial experiments. "According to the research to date, we use only five percent of our brain—the cerebral cortex—when we're thinking," she explains. "No one seems to know what happens to the other ninety-five percent, although part of it seems to function very well as a kind of tape recorder, storing up information about everything that has ever happened to us. Under hypnosis or sometimes with LSD it is possible to play back a "tape" starting from the first year of life—or even before—and progress through numerous experiences that have been totally forgotten.

"Some therapists and subjects—myself included—believe that it is possible to go even farther back beyond birth to other lives and actually bring back information about those existences. It is not at all uncommon for a subject under hypnosis to suddenly begin speaking a foreign language—a language totally unknown to him under ordinary circumstances. It's a simple matter for me at UCLA to send a tape over to the language department and have the so-called gibberish checked out. So much has come through this way that seems indicative of reincarnation.

"I know a young housewife who drew the floor plan of a most unusual house, unlike anything that she had ever seen before— or so she thought. It was a large home with numerous special details—far too expensive for her means at the time. So, reluctantly, she put away her blueprints and forgot about them. A few years later while exploring the ruins of Pompeii she came upon the exact same house. Each room was just as she had drawn it, right down to the last hallway.

"Now how can you explain this? Was the phenomen merely caused by a subconscious memory of a book read as a child and then long forgotten? Or had she actually lived a previous life in Pompeii? It's a little like the riddle of *The Lady or the Tiger?*, an unanswerable question. Did you read it somewhere or did it really happen? Unfortunately one can only find the answer by dying! In the meantime there's a living brain to consider with only a fraction of its activity accounted for. What goes on there? Some of us believe that this portion is the source of inspiration and creativity, which may be only a step away from healing power, ESP, or obtaining communication from the universal intelligence—the cosmic consciousness. It's not inconceivable that the brain acts like a radio receiver. The knowledge is simply there, and brains—in varying degrees—plug into it. We may all be linked together in an enormous range of unconscious knowledge.

"In this era of history, it appears that we are pulling away from the boundaries that have always confined us to this small earth. We are even now beginning to explore the regions that lie beyond outer space and within the atom. As we continue to probe the atom and the universe, we may find that there are a myriad of other dimensions to discover or rediscover. It may mean that this life, as we know it today, is just one experience among countless others."

Thelma Moss believes that the time has come to reevaluate the whole realm of religious experience. "If the mind does exist apart from the body in the sense that it can travel, then perhaps it can continue after the body ceases to exist," she conjectures. "Now that implies an immortal soul. This concept plunges us into the never-never land, the controversial area that few wish to discuss, of survival after death.

"Almost all the great religions postulate the existence

of life after death. And each of these religions has evolved from some remarkable person who lived in a different country at a different time in history and yet independently arrived at the concept of survival. This would seem to support Jung's idea of a universal unconscious. Should this collective phenomenon—belief in survival after death—prove to be a delusion, it would mean a good many persons, at different times in history, suffered the same delusion—which in itself is a fascinating thing to ponder."

As a result of her experiments and previous psychedelic experience, Thelma Moss the former cynic and materialist has come to believe in an ultimate, intelligent force. "I don't think there's any doubt of it," she says, "though I have no one particular religious belief and can't go along with organized religion. It's easier to view the force in physical terms. We are aware of the phenomenon of the atom, we know that atoms form into specific constellations to make a plant, an animal, a human being. And so we might view this atomic matter as the essence out of which everything rises; or, rather, the *energy* which infuses the atom. This energy is very likely the primal source— an idea shared for centuries by Zen Buddhists and by yogis before them.

"This idea of a fundamental energy or force could lead to the concept of thought or mind as the true creative force—a force that is constantly liable to obstruction by one's personal desires. They're a pretty common obstruction, wouldn't you say?"

Thelma Moss sees nothing new in the concept of surviving energy. "It's the second law of thermal dynamics," she points out. "Nothing is lost or gained in the whole universe. Why would we imagine that the life force within each person could be lost?

"*We die and something goes on living,* just try that idea on for size," she suggests. "There's such an immense legacy of fact and legend to which we can refer. Saint Paul, in the New Testament, wrote: 'There is a natural [physical] body and there is a spiritual body.' In the Tibetan *Book of the Dead,* specific instructions are left to the dying person on how to release the 'energy' body as death comes: 'When thou art recovered from the swoon [death] . . . a radiant body resembling the former body, must have sprung forth. This . . . is endowed with the power of miraculous motion.' Halfway around the world an amazingly similar—but apparently independent—guidebook came into being, *The Egyptian Book of the Dead.* Then there are numerous anecdotes of discarnate entities that apparently have not yet realized that they are 'dead.' The energies and desires of these earthbound spirits are still centered on earth so they remain here in a state of disorientation.

"It all comes back to the time-energy thing. If we make the assumption that there is such a thing as time, why not view it as energy that we can dip in and out of? We once thought of time as a straight line, but Einstein disproved that theory by establishing that time is curved. The analogy often used to explain the curvature of time is that of twin brothers, one of whom goes traveling through outer space for several years, and, upon returning home, discovers that he is considerably younger than his twin who remained on earth.

"Possibly our whole materialistic concept of time is wrong. Einstein once wrote, '*For us believing physicists, this separation between past, present and future has the value of mere illusion, however tenacious.*' It may be that our lives are recorded on a reel of film that may one day be played forward or backward. Moving backward in time, we could all be dinosaurs—moving forward, well, who knows? But is the dinosaur any less a reality than our present form? Is this instant any more real than the one before it or the next to follow?

"I think of this so often while watching my old friends and fellow actors of the late, late show. I'm twenty years older and many of them are 'dead.' But what does that really mean? Perhaps existence or reality as we know it is merely one instant in a constantly evolving process.

Bibliography

The Findhorn Foundation, *The Findhorn Garden*, (Moray, Scotland: Findhorn Publications).

The Findhorn Foundation, *Transformation of Findhorn*, (Moray, Scotland: Findhorn Foundation).

Paul Hawken, *The Magic of Findhorn*, (New York: Harper & Row, 1975).

Betty Bethards, *The Sacred Sword*, (Novato, Calif.: The Inner Light Foundation, 1972).

Betty Bethards, *Atlantis*, (Novato, Calif.: The Inner Light Foundation, 1974).

Rosemary Brown, *Unfinished Symphonies*, (New York: Bantam Books, Inc., 1972).

Stewart Robb, *New Music From Old Masters?*, *Psychic Magazine*, May, 1970

J.N. Sherwood, M.D., M.J. Stolaroff, and W.W. Harmon, Ph.D., 'The Psychedelic Experience—a New Concept in

Psychotherapy, *Journal of Neuropsychiatry*, Vol. 4, No. 2, December 1962.

Charles Savage, M.D., James Fadiman, Ph.D., Robert Mogar, Ph.D., and Mary Hughes Allen, M.D., *The Effects of Psychedelic (LSD) Therapy on Values, Personality and Behavior, International Journal of Neuropsychiatry*, Vol. 2, No. 3, May-June 1966.

Roberta DeLong Miller, *Psychic Massage*, New York: Harper Colophon Books, 1975.

Constance Newland, *My Self and I*, (New York: Coward McCann, Inc., 1962).

Thelma Moss, *The Probability of the Impossible* (Los Angeles: J. P. Tarcher, Inc., 1974).

"Interview: Thelma Moss," *Psychic Magazine*, August 1970.

Thelma Moss and J. A. Gengerelli, "Telepathy and Emotional Stimuli: A Controlled Experiment," *Journal of Abnormal Psychology*, 1967, Vol. 72, No. 4, pp. 341-48.

Alan Baron and Thomas G. Stampel, "A Note on 'Long Distance ESP': A Controlled Study," *Journal of Abnormal Psychology*, 1971, Vol. 78, No. 3, pp. 280-83.

Thelma Moss, "Reply to Baron and Stampel's 'A Note on Long Distance ESP': A Controlled Study," *Journal of Abnormal Psychology*, 1971, Vol. 78, No. 3, pp. 284-85.

Thelma Moss and Gertrude R. Schmeidler, "Quantitative Investigation of a 'Haunted House' with Sensitives and a Control Group," *Journal of the American Society for Psychical Research*, Vol. 62, No. 4, October 1968.